SKEPTICISM AND
MORAL PRINCIPLES

New University Press Studies in Ethics
and Society. Vol. I.

Thomas E. Wren, *General Editor*

Contributors for Vol. I:

Antony Flew

William Frankena

Marcus G. Singer

Skepticism and Moral Principles

Modern Ethics in Review

Edited with an introductory essay by

Curtis L. Carter

Published by New University Press, Inc.
P.O. Box 1534, Evanston, Illinois 60204

Library of Congress Card Number: 73–79477.

Printed in the United States of America.

The publisher wishes to thank Alfred A. Knopf, Inc. for permission
to reprint from the following:

H. D. Aiken, *Reason and Conduct*. ©1962, Alfred A. Knopf, Inc., N.Y.
Wallace Stevens, "Sketch of the Ultimate Politician," in *Collected
Poems* ©1954, Alfred A. Knopf, Inc., N.Y.

CONTENTS

NEW UNIVERSITY PRESS STUDIES IN ETHICS AND SOCIETY

FOREWORD BY THE GENERAL EDITOR

This series provides a forum for the critical review of enduring issues concerning ethics and society. This approach can be either direct, as in the discussion of skepticism in the present volume, or indirect, by discussing the positions of classical philosophers on these issues. In either case, however, the contributions are selected and introduced by the editor in a way most suitable for classroom use, either as a text-book or a supplementary reading.

After a period of malaise within and beyond the philosophical community, there is now fresh and extensive interest in evaluating personal and insti-tutional conduct. This series has been conceived in response to this new interest, but its contents are not to be regarded as if they had sprung fully formed from the brow of Zeus. It intends to provide contri-butors and readers alike with the opportunity for fresh and innovative philosophical thinking, but at the same time it recognizes that we see farther when we stand "on the shoulders of giants"—in this case, those of the great ethical and social philosophers of this and earlier centuries. Hence each contribution in the series is both a review and a proposal. Students and other non-professional philosophers may be more interested in the review, whereas professional philosophers will probably be more interested in the proposal, but in each contribution proposal and review require each other in order to be fully understood.

THOMAS E. WREN

SKEPTICISM AND MORAL THEORY IN CONTEMPORARY PHILOSOPHY

Introductory Essay[1]

Curtis L. Carter, Editor

Skepticism is the one problem above all others which has commanded the attention of moral philosophers in our century. Sometimes the problem is taken up explicitly, in full but uneasy consciousness; at others times it is treated indirectly, as in the troubled reflections from which emerge such questions as "Can moral principles be proved?" or "Is there a single 'right' point of view for confronting moral questions?" or "Why should I be moral at all?" In either case, skepticism as a moral view has never lacked vehement advocates or equally passionate and numerous opponents. Whereas earlier moral philosophers—such as nineteenth-century Idealists, whose views still influence thought in the twentieth century—proceeded on the assumption that moral values could be definitively established, contemporary British and American ethical theorists have tended to challenge that basic assumption. It may therefore, come as a surprise to many to find that the essays of this volume have been written in opposition to the generally dominant trend of twentieth-century skepticism.

I

"Skepticism" can be related to moral questions in three distinct ways: (1) as *skeptikos*, a thoughtful, inquiring investigation, probing, or testing; (2) as a habit of "a person who maintains a doubting attitude, as toward values, statements, or the character of others"; (3) as an intellectual position in relation to a set or sets of beliefs or principles, that is, a position to be taken and argued in relation to others, all of which claim some form of philosophical justification.[2]

The approach to skepticism as *skeptikos* is of interest to philosophers primarily as a method of inquiry. It has its usefulness for the investigation of moral questions as well as other sorts of questions, but it does not represent a developed intellectual position that would conflict with one or another position on morality. It is even compatible with at least some forms of moral absolutism. For its logical function is to lead to new information, clarification, and possibly to some principle or value or point of view which can serve as a firm basis for morality.

The second position—moral skepticism seen as personal doubting acting as a personality characteristic—is of less philosophical interest because it need not be anything more than an "unreasoned misanthropic state" or a view based on ignorance of fact or principle. To the extent that this view is of philosophical interest it can best be illuminated by direct attention to the more articulate forms of skepticism considered as an intellectual position.

The third approach to skepticism has special interest for moral philosophers, and is the one to which this book is addressed. In his contribution to this volume Marcus Singer characterizes moral skepticism as

> any theory that maintains that there can be no such thing as a good reason for a moral judgment, or that there are no valid moral arguments, or that ultimate moral principles cannot be proved, that morality has no rational basis, or that the difference between right and wrong is merely a matter of taste, opinion, feeling, or convention . . . .

This sets the limits for considering skepticism as a philosophical problem within the present context. And, since Singer's description covers both ancient and contemporary forms of skepticism, it also provides us with a useful tool for approaching the different forms and arguments of moral skepticism.

The question of moral skepticism can best be approached through its most completely articulated forms, as these are represented in currently prevailing philosophical theories. By naming and criticizing the different kinds of moral skepticism we can better understand their significance and their limitations. Moral skepticism is, of course, not a position which has been recently discovered or invented. It shows up in the writings of Greek sophists, evolutionary biologists, cultural anthropologists, Freudian psychologists, existentialist philosophers, and others.[3]

Earlier versions of moral skepticism suffer from generally "elusive and unsatisfactory" formulations, and do not distinguish clearly whether their skepticism is directed toward the entire moral enterprise or is limited to a prevailing moral code.[4] Some of the more recent versions of moral skepticism are the following: personal subjectivism, social subjectivism, ethical relativism, and the emotive theory of ethics, all of which are formulated and closely examined in the present essays.

However difficult it is to find a *philosophical* position of moral skepticism, we may at least state the criteria that such a view must fulfill. It would have to provide a fully articulated statement of the position, one that is clearly stated and free from obvious objections. The logical requirements of ordinary philosophic discourse such as conformity to the axiom of non-contradiction would have to be satisfied, and it would be necessary to delineate the kinds of ethical judgments which would be meaningful from a skeptical point of view. Moreover, a satisfactory statement of skepticism must specify whether the doubt concerns moral beliefs regarding a particular code or principle, all codes and principles, the possibility of achieving a rational basis for any morality, or something else. Finally, a well-formed statement of skepticism should provide evidence of having exerted sufficient rational effort to show the impossibility of "proving" or otherwise establishing a moral principle or a moral point of view.[5]

Since a position of moral skepticism is so difficult to formulate, even more difficult to defend, why is it such an attractive position to many philosophers in the present age? So far as I can see, the explanation of why they are attracted to it is to be found in these reasons. *First:* The fact that moral philosophers have failed to locate a single unproblematic moral principle on which everyone can agree, and from which action-guides can be derived for all moral behavior. *Second:* The uncritical ease with which one can argue from observable variations and disagreements in moral beliefs and practices among men, to the conclusion, comforting if unwarranted, that all values and all morality are equally without foundation or binding force. *Third:* Uncritical acceptance of scientific or pseudo-scientific empirical accounts of moral experience based on psychological, anthropological, and sociological interpretations. *Fourth:* Failure to appreciate the *fact* that certain aspects of morality require philosophical explanation and analysis which exceed the limits of empirical methodology. Misunderstanding of "scientific" treatments of moral experience results in a confusion of descriptive questions with normative ones and a consequent failure to distinguish the question of what people *do* believe or practice with what they *ought* to believe or practice. There are many episodes both in literature and in life which suggest that the morally ruthless person —Plato's "unjust man"—prospers while the morally serious or "just" man goes unrewarded for his fidelity to moral principles. *Fifth:* A failure to distinguish the question of *a* particular person's individual morality or *a* particular group's morality from the distinct question of *a moral point of view* from which all such *moralities* can be criticized. Relativism among *moralities* on certain points does not necessarily entail relativism for *the moral point of view*. At least it does not entail the forms of moral skepticism found in subjectivism, emotivism, and ethical relativism. *Sixth:* The ease of taking a position of moral skepticism as opposed to the rigorous working out of logical or other implications of a reasoned moral point of view makes the position popular with some of its advocates. Supporters in this category have undoubtedly given no more reasoned attention to skepticism than to other moral theories. Thus in some cases skepticism is arrived at by default, by the failure to investigate sufficiently the possibilities of finding rationally defensible or "true" moral principles which are the result of moral deliberation.

II

The essays by William Frankena, Marcus Singer, and Antony Flew which follow address themselves to the above considerations. One or more of these "attractive" features is critically examined by each essay.

Fankena examines the current state of moral principles in the light of cultural hostility to the idea of morality, and argues for a sense of true morality seen from "the moral point of view" and representing a distinct human enterprise. Contrary to the prevailing attitudes of moral skepticism and relativism, Frankena distinguishes a moral point of view from a particular morality, that is, a particular set of moral beliefs, rules, and practices. There can be moral principles which are absolutes within the moral point of view, whereas the specific rules or practices may well be relative. Frankena thus seeks to deprive moral skepticism of one of its most persuasive arguments by clarifying the relation between the idea of *moralities*, in which some variations in rules and practices may be found, and the notion of the moral point of view—which is absolute. Thus individual and group moralities are not the final ground of judgment, and their rules and practices are subject to review from the "moral point of view."

Applying the term "moral skepticism" to established philosophical views, Singer characterizes four versions: personal subjectivism, social subjectivism, emotivism, and the social pressure theory of obligation.[6] He also cites as *sources* of moral skepticism the positions of egoism and determinism. A criticism of moral skepticism is its generally elusive and indeterminate character. Singer clarifies this weakness by stating the moral problem of skepticism in concrete terms and by giving concrete examples. Having pinned down significant examples, he sets to work on them with the fine tools of logical analysis. His critique of each form of skepticism is based on strict logical procedure, so that his closely reasoned refutation exposes the fallacies and contradictions within the various skeptical arguments. He shows that the different forms of moral skepticism collapse into logical fallacies and absurdities. Singer deals specifically with three forms of moral skepticism: that predicated upon the alleged reliability of individual or social group attitudes, that which argues from diversity or disagreement concerning moral beliefs, and that which defines moral judgments as expressions of feelings or persuasive utterances. Singer concludes that despite their attractiveness, all these forms of skepticism are ultimately without validity.

Finally, Flew undertakes a fresh examination of the ancient sophists' skeptical thesis, represented by Thrasymachus in the *Republic*, that the life of the unjust man is superior to that of the just man. Flew shows that in its source the sophists' doctrine is completely contemporary. Taking on Socrates, Flew agrees with Thrasymachus that the life of the unjust man is more advantageous than the life of the just man. But he confronts skepticism by showing that the person who expects to be rewarded for moral behavior has misunderstood the nature of morality. In the light of recent discussions in moral philosophy, Flew brings fresh insight to the question concerning just actions and reward. He goes beyond Socrates' apparently true but not always comforting assurance that just behavior contains its own intrinsic reward. To the question "Must morality pay?" Flew replies that Thrasymachus is right in his empirical observation that the just man is not always rewarded. Justice cannot be defined in terms of any special individual or group interests. Because of this, morality often demands sacrifices, as when the collective interest and the individual interest come into conflict. Therefore, the proper understanding of

morality as distinct from self-interest eliminates the
ground for moral skepticism arising from the challenge of Thrasymachus' observations.

III

In his essay, "The Principles of Morality,"
Frankena expounds his original conception, developed in previous essays, that ethical theory should
be considered within the larger context of "the moral
institution of life." This approach enables us, he
believes, "to grasp the nature of morality itself, as
compared with law, religion, science." Art, prudence, and education are also mentioned in Frankena's essays.[7] His previous essays have approached
the question of morality by identifying and analyz-
ing differing points of view on these matters and by
examining morality relative to action-guides that
are "moral" as opposed to non-moral or immoral.

In his article "Recent Conceptions of Morality,"
Frankena classifies current moral theories according
to their uses of individualist, formalist, or social
criteria to describe the nature of morality, and tells
us that a morality must include both trans-indi-
vidual social considerations as well as logical rational
ones.[8] The discussion of the question "What is
morality?" is advanced in "The Concept of Morality," where he asks, "When is an individual or
society to be said to have a morality or a moral action-guide?", or "When is a code or action-guide to
be called a moral one, a morality?" An action-guide
consisting of "moral" rules and beliefs is acceptable

as a moral one when it meets certain requirements:
(1) The action-guide must be taken by a person as a
prescriptive statement, or one which implies that
the person *ought* to abide by the rules of the action-
guide. (2) The person acting as a moral agent uni-
versalizes the action-guide, meaning that he believes
it is applicable to others in similar circumstances.
(3) The person believes that the action-guide or its
principles are overriding, supremely authoritative
principles. (4) Finally, the person believes that a set
of material conditions which spell out the probable
effects of abiding by the action-guide is required of
a satisfactory moral action-guide.[9] All of these act
as a set of criteria for distinguishing a morality
from something else.

In his contribution to this volume, namely, "The
Principles of Morality," Frankena considers morality
in its general function as one of several related areas
of human interest. He remarks that when we discuss
morality as a particular human enterprise we use
both relativistic phrases such as "the morality of the
Chinese," with the suggestion that "morality" refers to "something that is variable and changeable,"
and also phrases like "the moral law," which "appear to refer to something that is absolute and
unchanging." Noting that the distinction between
relativistic and absolute uses of morality has been
somewhat neglected in the present mood of pluralism, Frankena develops his earlier discussions of the
relative and variable senses of "morality" by analyz-
ing the absolutist meanings of "morality." He identifies eight distinct views which attempt to explain

the meaning of "what morality requires," "the supreme principles of morality," etc., and then proposes what may well be the strongest version of ethical absolutism to be found in any contemporary British or American philosopher. Because his attack on moral skepticism depends upon taking an absolutist "moral point of view," it is important to understand Frankena's moral point of view clearly, for the absolute moral principles that emanate from it are Frankena's counter to skepticism. (His previous essays contain somewhat more brief statements of the meaning Frankena here gives to the moral point of view.)

The moral point of view can be characterized as follows: It is one of several points of view which include those taken in science, art, law, and education, and a person acting from this point of view must be free, fully informed, and clear-headed. When he is acting rationally under these conditions he acts from a point of view which transcends his own moral attitudes or those of his society.[10] Or as he defines it in another, more technical explanation, the moral point of view is a canon of "good reasons," consisting of rules of relevance which indicate what is significant from the point of view, and rules of inference for making valid moral judgments.[11]

Acting from the moral point of view means taking a view and claiming that other rational men who are taking the moral point of view will agree. The agreement is expressed in having similar moral attitudes, performing the same moral acts, and making judgments based on the principles connected with the point of view.[12] In addition to these characteristics, he suggests this analogy in "The Principles of Morality": morality "tells" or "teaches" us in somewhat the same way as do science and history. This is an amplification of the previously noted point that the moral point of view is like points of view in science, history, and other institutions. This latest version compares the force of moral utterances with the force of statements based on points of view known to be taken as authoritative by many people.

Frankena goes on to introduce a requirement of first-person involvement, whereby the moral agent takes responsibility for the rationality of the acts performed from the moral point of view. In short, the true principles of the moral point of view are discovered or revealed but are not created, invented, or established by acts of decision and commitment.

The principles may *not* turn out to be the true principles of the moral point of view. But a person is rationally justified in acting on the principles he is led to accept when he is taking the moral point of view: that is, when he attempts to act in clearheaded and logical fashion, with full information about the facts. This qualification may open the door to the possibility of some element of skepticism, but skepticism does not necessarily follow. Like the scientist, the moral person—a person, that is, who takes the moral point of view—subscribes in intent or promise to the findings of his method. Accordingly, he stands ready to correct his principles whenever the evidence (such as disagreement by ideal observers) warrants revision. Disagreement over *the principles of morality* is thus possible, but evidently there is, according to Frankena, only one true set of moral principles. Hence there exists a strong probability that the principles one arrives at from the moral point of view will be sustained by future reconsiderations. There is thus no room for subjectivist or relativist views of morality.

Against the claim of moral skepticism that we can never say with justification that some actions or principles are right or true, Frankena asserts that by taking the moral point of view a person *can* know this with all reasonable certainty.

Has Frankena succeeded in countering the movement which led relativists like E. Westermarck to conclude that the alleged objective foundations of morality are in shambles,[13] or that which prompted emotivists to the conclusion that ethical statements are merely expressions of feeling with no objective ground?[14] Not all readers of his essay will agree that Frankena has been so successful. His critics will fall into two broad groups—those who agree with Frankena on the possibility of a moral point of view but would not accept Frankena's account of it, and those who deny the possibility of any sort of meaningful notion of *the moral point of view*. In his critical review of moral theories that might pose as alternatives to his own position, Frankena has in fact anticipated both of these lines of attack. He points out their deficiencies, particularly in the views of R. Linton, R. Firth, and H. Aiken.

Ascribing to Linton the view that "morality" in such phrases as "the principles of morality" means "the totality of all norms actually accepted universally by all cultures," Frankena objects that such a view fails to distinguish what is from what ought to be.[15] Whereas the moral point of view is concerned with the totality of rationally justified moral norms that *should* govern the moral life, Linton's view would provide only a summary of prevailing norms. Linton fails to present a criterion from which to criticize adequately either particular moralities or the "set of universally agreed upon principles." It is therefore deficient as a possible account of the moral point of view.

Frankena also takes notice of the Ideal Observer theory of the moral point of view. This theory, proposed by R. Firth, holds that true moral principles are justified by the fact that it would be approved by a person or God (Ideal Observer) who looked at the moral principle or moral act from a position of omniscience, omnipercipience, disinterestedness, dispassionateness, and logical consistency.[16] This ethical theory is similar in important respects to Frankena's, in that the two theories have in common a commitment to moral objectivism. However, an advocate of the Ideal Observer theory would perhaps object to Frankena's insistence on first-person involvement. To an Ideal Observer involvement violates the conditions of objectivity implied in the criteria of "dispassionate" or "disinterested" spectator approaches. To this Frankena would probably reply by restating the objections he has expressed in this book concerning the suitability of these criteria. Since his own and the Ideal Observer theory share a common agreement about the absolutism of moral principles, their disagreement is primarily over the involvement of the appropriate attitude of the moral agent, and over the definition of the Ideal Observer.

A third position is Kurt Baier's view of the moral point of view. Scant mention of Baier occurs in Frankena's paper, but Baier's view deserves still more attention with reference to Frankena's paper. For Baier clearly recognizes the distinction between *moralities* and *the moral point of view*.[17] As he sees it the difference between them is that particular moral codes or parts of them are subject to review from "the point of view of morality." Baier recognizes the difference but apparently does not know quite what to do with it. Commenting on the distinction between one and another morality and "true morality," he says,

> Let us be quite clear, however, what this distinction amounts to. It is not, in the first place, that between "a morality" and "morality as such," which is analogous to the distinction between a legal system and law as such . . . . Talking about a morality, say Greek . . . , is like talking about Roman . . . law. But talking about morality as such or the nature of morality is like talking about law as such. . . . When talking in this way, we are drawing attention to the essentials of the concept. We are thinking of the conditions which something must satisfy in order to be properly called "a morality" . . . . Morality as such is not a super-mortality, . . .

not even a morality, but a set of conditions. Morality as such cannot therefore be either true or false. . . . There is no prior reason to assume that there is only one true morality. There are many moralities and of these a large number happen to pass the test which moralities must pass in order to be true.[18]

But then Baier goes on to say that there *is* a sense in which we can speak of "true morality." This would be a system true for all possible social conditions, but taken in abstraction from actual true moralities, those systems which meet the criteria for any true moral system.[19]

> I shall then distinguish between true moralities and absolute morality. True moralities are actually embodied moralities, those forming part of a given way of life of a society or an individual, which would pass a certain test if they were subjected to it. Absolute morality, on the other hand is that set of moral convictions, whether held by anyone or not, which is true quite irrespective of any particular social conditions in which they might be embodied.[20]

There is clearly some confusion on Baier's part concerning morality. As it stands, the "test" for true moral codes is extracted from those codes that are being tested or that *have been tested*. But tested by what criteria?[21] The difficulty results from the fact that Baier has no independent basis upon which to establish criteria. Baier's requirements for the moral point of view can be stated succinctly: He asks that one adopt as a supreme, overriding principle the agreement to abide by moral rules which are for the good of everyone alike. However, because the operational basis for defining the principles of morality is itself circular, by being composed of principles abstracted from actual moralities, Baier fails to come up with an independent set of rules for characterizing *the principles of morality*. He is thus lacking an objective base for the principles attached to the moral point of view.

In contrast, Frankena understands the moral point of view as taken from the perspective of morality as an institution alongside others such as science, religion, and art. Whereas Baier denies the possibility of an "ideal standard of morality as such," which can also be a "true" morality, Frankena asserts his belief in the ideal true moral principles of the moral point of view. The principles are true because of the manner in which they are arrived at, because they conform to rational human nature, and ultimately because rational human nature happens to be in conformity or harmony with the rational nature of the universe.[22] Hence by treating the moral point of view as an absolute, Frankena provides for the possibility of independent criteria. These criteria consist of true moral principles which can be used as a test of individual or social moral beliefs—an element lacking in Baier's theory of the moral point of view. Consequently, Baier's "absolute morality" refers not to Frankena's absolutism in the moral point of view, but rather to something closer to Linton's universally agreed upon moral principles. Nevertheless, Baier himself would probably object to Frankena's notion of absolute moral principles which represent true morality.[23]

Philippa Foot has presented a thesis which resembles Frankena's account of the moral point of view,[24] although it does so only approximately. Unlike Frankena, she considers the moral point of view as optional, contingent on current beliefs of the moral agent, and only subjectively and conditionally necessary. However, she seems to agree that "oughts" can arise with respect to a moral point of view.

> My own conclusion is that "One ought to be moral" makes no sense at all unless the "ought" has the moral subscript, giving a tautology, or else relates morality to some other system such as prudence or etiquette. I am therefore putting forward quite seriously a theory that disallows the possibility of saying that a man ought (free unsubscripted "ought") to have ends other than he does have; e.g., that the uncaring, amoral man ought to care about the relief of suffering or the protection of the weak. In my view we must start from the fact that some people do care about such things, and even talk about what should be done presupposing common aims.[25]

Foot asserts that men do not necessarily have

moral ends; that they happen to have them is a voluntary matter, subject to change as their desires change. A claim to binding force for moral principles—Frankena's true principles of the moral point of view are binding for rational men—is therefore suspect. Arguing for a voluntary approach to morality, Foot says.

> Many people feel uneasy about the things that are said about the authority and binding force of morality, fearing like Thrasymachus that they may be being tricked. In my view their skepticism is well grounded, since I believe that many of the statements with which people would bolster the "authority" of the "moral law" are in fact meaningless, unless viewed as expressions of the *feeling* that we have about morality. As stating what we tend to feel they make sense; taken in any other way they do not.[26]

The basic point of disagreement between Frankena and Foot is over the nature and significance of the tautology by which she characterizes a moral ought which derives from a moral point of view. The conclusion of radical skepticism at which Foot arrives is based on two questionable arguments: (1) her claim that moral oughts based on a point of view are tautologies, (2) her assertion that the force of moral laws derives from the feelings people have about them. Neither of these arguments is decisive. The charge that "oughts" derived from a moral point of view are tautologies—that is, are based on rules which do not necessarily exclude any possibilities—is relevant only if moral principles are understood as components in systems analogous to formal logical or mathematical models. Frankena's adoption of the methodology of a point of view is based on analysis deriving from a system of "value logic." The system Frankena uses was proposed by Paul Taylor and is intended to justify value judgments in normative discourse. It goes beyond the theory of verification and validation operative in the empirical sciences and formal logical systems.[27] A point of view such as the moral one is defined in terms of its own rules of relevance and valid inference. Foot or anyone else who advances the tautology thesis has to agree that not all rules of logic and inference which hold for the empirical sciences are *necessarily* applicable in the context of the moral point of view. Considerations which do not apply to points of view wherein moral judgments and values in general are not at issue. Moreover, even if the charge of tautology against a moral point of view such as Frankena's can be sustained it is not decisive, provided that the tautology is real. Frankena postulates a connection between morality and rationality, which asserts that the "tautology" is supported by man's rational nature and ultimately by the fact that man's rationality is validated by the rational nature of the universe. As for the argument from the way people feel, this has never carried much philosophical weight because of the impossibility of measuring feelings and assessing their import. I see no reason to give significant weight to feeling in this case either.

Beyond these objections to Frankena's thesis based on a notion different from his of the moral point of view itself, there are criticisms from those who simply deny that real moral judgments can be based on this point of view. Chief among such critics are H. Aiken, J. Rachels, and of course those who hold positions of normative or meta-ethical relativism.[28] Not all who deny the possibility of a moral point of view with absolute principles would see the alternative as skepticism. As Frankena here shows, Aiken rejects the moral point of view with its moral absolutism on the grounds that such a view is incompatible with the principle of moral autonomy, which Aiken takes as a more fundamental notion. In contrast to Frankena, his definition of "moral objectivity" includes three elements, the first of which is a denial of the supposition that objective principles require some universal standard or practice of right and wrong which is acknowledged as binding by all men of good will. The second calls for readjustment of moral objectivity to provide for the possibility of an essential diversity of moral codes; and a third redefines moral objectivity in the context of workaday moral problems. Thus moral objectivity becomes a "piecemeal mutual adjustment of acknowledged commitments, a loose framework of precepts and practices, none of which is ever permanently earmarked as an absolutely first principle and each of which is subject to a list of exceptions that can never be exhaustively stated."[29]

Rachels is a critic of those moral theories which try to build on the idea of a point of view. His recent survey of such theories makes a concentrated attack on these theories, including Frankena's, by arguing that moral judgments cannot be made from within a point of view, because in fact there is no such thing as a moral point of view.[30] It is not necessary to examine the entire sequence of arguments offered by Rachels to show that his criticisms of Frankena's view are without warrant. His critique defines the moral point of view as a set of interests,[31] but this is not the explanation which Frankena gives. He in fact has never defined the moral point of view in any strict sense at all. His description of it cited earlier in this essay suggests a different concern. Whereas Rachels' account speaks of the content of the moral point of view—a set of interests—Frankena's descriptions suggest rather an attempt to discover moral principles and a means of validating moral judgments—all this in accordance with canons of reasoning appropriate to the point of view.[32]

To the extent that Frankena's comments on the moral point of view indicate any significant concern with content, this concern is directed toward the absolute and rational moral principles connected with the point of view. The "interests" in this case, if broad fundamental principles of justice and benevolence can properly be designated as interests, are not on the level of the sort of interests discussed by Rachels. They are not the special interests of self-interested persons or groups. Nor are they at the level of the farmer's point of view or the film maker's.

Rather they apply equally to all.[33] I conclude that Rachels has not destroyed the foundations of the notion of a moral point of view in this article. Rather it appears that his own arguments rest on a misreading of the moral point of view.[34]

A central thesis of most modern forms of skepticism about the possibility of establishing any absolute moral point of view is the claim that the "facts" of cultural relativism necessarily entail some form of ethical relativism. This may express itself as a *normative* relativism, according to which "what is right or good for one individual or society need not be right or good for another even when the situations in question are similar"; or as a *meta-ethical* relativism, which maintains that "there can be no sound procedures for justifying one moral code or one set of moral judgments as over against another . . . ."[35] While the belief that these two forms of ethical relativism follow from cultural relativism was once held to be nearly self-evidently true, this is no longer the case. Anthropologists such as C. Kluckhohn are now inclined to argue that both cultural relativism and the ethical relativism that derives from it are false.[36] Such philosophers as K. Nielsen have argued that even if the facts of cultural relativism were true, they would not be sufficient to establish ethical relativism of either kind without the additional support of powerful theoretical considerations.[37]

The arguments of both Frankena and Singer in their respective essays support the above reservations concerning normative ethical relativism. They may also provide some ground for a critique of meta-ethical relativism; and this form of moral skepticism is the more troublesome, for if it can be sustained, the advocates of moral skepticism will find considerable support. From the assumed premises "that dissimilar cultures use different methods of reasoning to justify moral claims," and "that there are no universal criteria in virtue of which we could determine which method or methods are sound," the meta-ethical relativists conclude that the very basis for any absolute moral point of view has been destroyed.[38]

But the main problem with this line of reasoning is (or has been) a lack of sufficiently refined systems of cross-cultural categories for determining whether the thought categories are really different, or whether there is an underlying similarity of concept categories for approaching moral problems. Until the cross-cultural categories are established it cannot be determined that apparent cultural diversity either supports or denies normative or meta-ethical relativism.

Is the "moral point of view" a cross-cultural category? Taylor states that it is, and presumably Frankena agrees.[39] If they are correct, we have made more progress than is suggested by Nielsen's cautious though sympathetic attitude toward the possibility of achieving common principles and a common method of reasoning. One who believes that a true morality *is* possible may also be encouraged by the fact that cultural anthropologists provide grounds neither for affirmining nor denying such claims.

IV

Singer's critical examination of moral skepticism in the present volume has its beginning in his *Generalization in Ethics*, where he devotes a few pages to ethical relativism, that is, the theory that all moral ideas are necessarily relative to a given society. Singer judges the position to be fallacious because it overlooks an important distinction between moral principles and moral rules. Rules may be relative in certain circumstances, but moral principles are "universal in scope." Fundamental moral rules are only relative in the sense that they are not binding under certain circumstances.[40]

In the essay in this volume, entitled "Moral Skepticism," Singer concisely distinguishes and defines each of the four types of moral skepticism. *Moral subjectivism* is of two kinds, personal and social. *Personal subjectivism* holds that moral judgments are attitudes of approval or disapproval of individuals, whereas *social subjectivism* treats them as questions of group approval or disapproval. The *emotive theory* interprets moral judgments not as statements capable of being true or false but as expressions of feeling having only "emotive meaning." The *social pressure* theory defines moral obligation as a feeling of compulsion resulting from social pressure or the desire to conform. *Ethical relativism*, finally, is the position defined above.

Beyond these specific forms of moral skepticism, Singer further identifies two sources of moral skepticism: psychological egoism and determinism. *Psychological egoism* is the view that everyone acts for

his own interest, and *determinism* maintains that anyone's behavior is caused by factors independent of
the person's control.[41]

Having provided examples of moral skepticism
and its causes, Singer devotes the major portion of
the essay to an analysis and critique of the subjectivist and emotive theories. Singer has little regard
for either form of subjectivism. The value in discussing them is derived from the criticisms by which
Singer hopes to illuminate the question of judgments
of right or wrong. The major objection to personal
subjectivism is that it makes nonsense of such serious
moral questions as, "Is this action right or wrong?"
by reducing them to the totally subjective query,
"Do I approve or disapprove of this action?" Such
reduction ends in a confusion which fails to make
sense of moral questions, offers no guidance toward
answering the original question, "Is this right?",
and contradicts the fact that moral philosophers and
other persons do engage in disagreements which
cannot be settled by appeal to individual attitudes
for approval or disapproval.[42]

Social subjectivism is objectionable because it
turns moral criticisms of the community by a mem-
ber of that community into contradictory or senseless statements. Social subjectivism involves a confusion between the *fact* that we may (and often do)
acquire moral beliefs from the community in which
we live, and the quite distinct critical question as to
the *meaning* these beliefs contain, either in themselves
or with reference to ourselves. Its popularity is thus
based on erroneous reasoning just as was the attrac-

tiveness of personal subjectivism.

The emotive theory, whose principal exponents include Ayer and Stevenson, was developed to answer the objections to subjectivism.[43] Singer views the emotive theory as a more interesting, more sophisticated form of skepticism. Its principal importance is to call attention to the significance of attitudes and feelings in moral experience. Although the emotive theory purports to account for certain facts about morality, it does not in fact provide reasons to support its principal claims: that ethical concepts are unanalyzable, and that the emotive theory uniquely accounts for certain facts of moral experience. These facts are alleged to be the widespread theoretical disagreement on ethical questions, and the frequent, often abusive disputes that arise over the matters of fact in a moral situation. Singer denies that these "facts" are pertinent facts or unique to moral experience, so that the facts emotive theory is trying to account for are non-facts. Moreover, the emotive theory fails to explain adequately the *real* facts of moral experience. The emotive theory leaves logical relationships between ethical statements inexplicable. It precludes the giving of reasons in support of moral judgments and is thus morally irrelevant. Finally the statement, "This is good," is incompletely translated into the sentence: "I approve of this: do so as well." In like manner a translation of "Is X good?" into a request for influence will not work in all cases, as when the moralist asks the question of himself.

Singer's arguments against subjectivism and the

emotive theory do not actually *disprove* either of the two points of view. To accomplish this complete refutation requires the additional step of a positive basis for moral judgments, an admittedly more arduous task, which Singer has taken up elsewhere.[44] In the present essay, he does however argue, forcefully and convincingly, that if either subjectivism or the emotive theory is taken or accepted as the "correct" theory of moral experience, the "facts" of moral experience, when viewed logically and rationally, are left in an extremely untidy state.

In opposition to Singer's analysis is the attempt of D. H. Monro to show the reasonableness of subjectivism or relativism.[45] Critics of subjectivism and relativism, he argues, confuse an argument based on appeal to error in belief with disagreement over taste or desire. Error in belief is an "intellectual error" which, if an honest mistake, is not subject to moral condemnation. Disagreement in taste or desire, says Monro, *is*, however, a legitimate ground from which the subjectivist or relativist may issue moral condemnation. The denial of the relativist's right to condemn actions "by reason of" disagreement over taste is inappropriate, argues Monro, because it supposes that disagreement in matters of taste can be equated with some form of intellectual error. The denial is based on the principle that false beliefs and only false beliefs are to be rejected. He argues that the moral relativist cannot in fairness be required to abide by a principle which is incompatible with his own basic relativism. In the past, moral objectivists who believed in moral absolutes criticized subjectivists and relativists for basing moral judgments on individual or group attitudes.

Monro tries to place subjectivist-relativist advocates on equal ground with objectivists by suggesting that the moral beliefs of objectivists are also really attitudes in disguise. The objectivist condemns actions on the basis of beliefs concerning the truth of rational moral principles, while the subjectivist-relativist condemns them on the basis of disagreement over attitude. Neither has an advantage for criticism of the other if Monro is correct. But is he? Singer has shown in the essay contributed here that statements reflecting moral beliefs have such logical relations as entailment. The same cannot be said for subjective statements of attitude. Statements of belief can be true or false. Statements of attitude cannot be understood in the same way. There are thus differences between belief and attitude that appear to preclude the reduction of beliefs to attitudes.

Intriguing as Monro's argument is, it seems less than convincing in other ways as well; Singer has shown, for instance, that the subjectivist or relativist account of moral experience is inadequate. Moreover, the subjectivist-objectivist position can be defended against the charge of pure arbitrariness only if it is seen as dependent on a set of naturalist assumptions, chief among them the implied assertion that moral agents act by reference to a set of ends mutually agreed to. A point played down in Monro's argument is that there is *no reason* that a subjectivist could offer for his moral judgments in the expectation that others *ought* to share his attitudes, hence no basis for assuming that they *will*. The appeal to an inner urge to make moral attitudes consistent, whether one's own or the community's, does not follow from the more basic subjectivist or relativist presupposition that the basis for moral judgment is individual or social attitudes. Another possible alternative for avoiding the arbitrariness attached to skepticism or relativism is found in Monro's suggestion that attitudes are forced upon persons by a combination of psychological and social forces.[46] But this explanation is also inadequate, since it converts the subjectivist criterion—the attitudes of an individual or a group—into a form of determinism, and these two theories, as we have remarked above, are not the same. Attitudes have been replaced by blind inner or external forces which are completely out of the realm of rational control.

Singer would agree with Frankena that there are true moral principles. He arrives at his own version of true, ultimate rational moral principles through examination of the generalization principle, which in turn derives from an examination of the moral force of the question, "What would happen if everyone did that?" Generalization and other moral principles are worked out in detail in Singer's book, *Generalization in Ethics*.[47] This view can only be noted in passing here, but it offers another "defense" of absolutism in moral principles complementary to Frankena's.

V

Flew's essay, "Must Morality Pay? . . ." is a critical re-examination of Socrates' attempt, long accepted as a definitive refutation of the moral skepticism of the sophists, to show that just action is, after
all, advantageous to the just man. Flew notes that
no one is really satisfied with Socrates' answer because it fails to come to grips with the distinction
between what *is* the case and what *ought* to be the
case. The latter point has become highly visible in
the writings of twentieth-century philosophers, especially in light of G. E. Moore's attack on the
"naturalistic fallacy," which is the attempt to define
"good" and "right" in terms of such natural qualities as "pleasure" or "advantage."[48] Flew's concern
is not merely to reinterpret the dispute between
Thrasymachus and Socrates as an is-ought question,
but to show how the semantic and conceptual deficiencies that he uncovers in the ancient debate are
of great importance to contemporary disagreements
about the meaning and nature of justice and other
moral absolutes. The result is a reinterpretation
which clarifies the relation of just actions and reward
viewed from a moral point of view as distinct from
the view of self-interest.[49]

The substantive issue of concern to Socrates and
Thrasymachus centers on Thrasymachus' assertion
that the life of the unjust man is superior to the life
of the just man. Thrasymachus sees that being just

involves sacrifice of one's own material interests to
the interests of others. He reasons that being just
under these conditions is foolish, and that injustice
is at least good practical policy. Moreover, Thrasymachus *knows* that good men are often short-changed
and that men who act solely for their own advantage
are rewarded handsomely. This is so even when they
exhibit rampant disregard for the interests of others.
Socrates, on the other hand, expresses his position
in the classic paradox that the supposed advantage
of the unjust man is really misery, whereas the apparent disadvantages experienced by the man who
lives according to justice work ultimately to his
good. The result is two sharply opposing views.

How can the two conclusions be so different? The
difference follows from the fact that Socrates and
Thrasymachus, who appear to be proceeding from
the same starting point, are actually *not* taking the
same starting point at all. Each has a different concept of advantage or reward, and thus each starts
from different sides of the is-ought perspective. Socrates understands advantage as intrinsic value. Actions are thus advantageous or not as they enhance
the quality of life. Just actions are in effect self-
rewarding, whereas unjust actions have a negative
reward. This negative reward consists of a failure to
realize the good, and a corresponding debilitation
of character. On this understanding morality cannot help but be rewarded. Thrasymachus, on the
other hand, sees reward as visible success, prosperity,
in effect material well-being. He gives little thought
to the quality of human life apart from these con-

siderations, though he would probably agree that if everyone were to act justly the situation would be to the common good.

The points of view of Socrates and Thrasymachus also differ in the way they perceive the question of justice. Speaking for Plato, Socrates arrives at his answer by referring to an ideal of what *ought* to be the case. Thrasymachus, on the other hand, responds from an empirical standpoint of what, in brute fact, is the reality of human experience. Hence they are not relating to the question from the same point of view. Thrasymachus sees the issue as a descriptive matter, Socrates as a normative one.

The differences between Socrates and Thrasymachus do not end with their disagreement over the nature of advantage or reward, nor with their separate approaches to the question of morality from an "ought" or "is" perspective. Also at issue is a disagreement over the definition of "justice." Thrasymachus tries at first to say that justice is a *relative* concept whose meaning varies as it is defined in different contexts or by different persons. The variable contexts in his examples are different forms of government. Rulers in a dictatorship define justice so that it works to the advantage of the government, and so do aristocracies and democracies. The result is that justice turns out to be the advantage of the established power structure.

In the exchange between Socrates and Thrasymachus there is a constant shift in the supposition and understanding of "justice"—to Socrates it means the moral ideal which should obtain among good men, to Thrasymachus it parades as an artificial convention agreed on by weak men as protection against the evil they recognize in men as they are. This ambivalence results because they lack the necessary conceptual tools to treat properly the question of justice. At first Socrates takes Thrasymachus' definition to be a descriptive definition of justice. He responds properly though inadequately with a factual reply. But then, as the discussion continues, Thrasymachus states that he is making a thesis about the actual behavior of men in power. Socrates replies with a speculative hypothetical statement "that rulers *may* by mistake command what happens not in fact to be in their interests." This statement functions primarily as a rhetorical retort, and leads the discussion astray. At this point Thrasymachus goes off on other irrelevant normative speculation by giving a stipulative definition of a true ruler as one who can make no such mistake.

The outcome is that the resolution of their difficulties is beyond the conceptual and linguistic facility given to Socrates and Thrasymachus by Plato. It turns out that neither Socrates nor Thrasymachus possesses the philosophical skill to recognize the conceptual difficulties involved. Statements of both Socrates and Thrasymachus shift back and forth between the factual (is) and the normative (ought) perspectives during the debate. Flew suggests that Thrasymachus' thesis that justice is the interest of the stronger should not be taken as a semantic analysis of "justice." Rather it can best be understood as an attempt to analyze a state of affairs, what is actually going on. Otherwise, the linguistic confusions make impossible the resolution of the controversy over the meaning of justice, and fail to deliver the desired insight into justice and into the nature of morality in a more general sense.

The debate also brings out an important substantive point which is missed by Socrates: that Thrasymachus is defining justice in terms of special individuals or group interests. Here begins Flew's answer to the question raised in the title of his essay, "Must Morality Pay? Or, What Socrates Should Have Said To Thrasymachus." In effect, this reply should have been that justice or morality cannot be defined as the interests of individuals or groups at all. If morality is to provide principles for impartially settling conflicts of interest, the principles must not be stated in reference to any special interests. This restriction applies not only to justice but to all moral principles that are to provide relevant guidance in answering the question, "What ought I to do?" It follows that from the moral point of view all persons must have equal claim to fair consideration of their respective interests. But if the moral principles themselves bear the stamp of some special interest, so that in fact they exclude opposed interests, the very statement of such qualified principles must lead to moral skepticism about the possibility of absolute principles.

Thrasymachus is right when he asserts that in the empirical situation—that is, in life as men actually live it in the real world—justice is not always rewarded and injustice often produces personal gain.

Since morality cannot be identified with individual
or group interests, the just man may have to pay for
his justice by sacrificing his personal interests to the
interests of others. Since we do not in fact live in the
ideal world that Socrates envisions as a philosophic
possibility for those who have seen the Forms of
justice and goodness, there can be no assurance of
justice being rewarded. It would be misguided to
try to meet Thrasymachus's observations with a
denial of the empirical situation.

Socrates might of course reply that in his own
proposed commonwealth of men who are just in
virtue of their knowledge of the absolute Form of
Justice, the "empirical" situation would be quite
different: in *that* human context, observance of the
principle of justice would really guarantee the common good.[50] But that hypothesis is *not* the issue
between Socrates and Thrasymachus, nor in any
debate about justice in the real world peopled by
real men. In this world, the empirical fact is that
individual and group interests do not always coin-
cide; indeed, that the common good is often in stark
opposition to the good which the individual proposes for himself. The truth, says Flew, is that
morality demands sacrifices. This point is concealed
in Plato's analysis of justice in the *Republic*.

However, Flew's analysis seems to take too little
account of Socrates' distinction between intrinsic
and extrinsic good. Socrates could reply, "Yes. I
concede the point you are making from Thrasymachus' point of view. But I have a different conception of advantage, one based on the notion of

intrinsic value. Just actions are worth doing for their own sake or for the enhancement of character which results from their being done. This is sufficient reward for the moral man." Glaucon demands that Socrates show what justice is "in itself, within the soul of the just man." That it produces an "advantage" is true; but this consists of the interior beauty and health of the soul which justice and the other virtues work therein. And, as Socrates demonstrated in his own life, he intends *this* statement as applicable even to the "empirical" situation which Thrasymachus is describing.

If Socrates chose to reply in this manner, it would be impossible to refute his point by appeal to empirical conditions of material advantage. Moreover, if it is the case that Socrates and Thrasymachus do take different approaches to the question of advantage, Socrates' reply is a perfectly proper one.

VI

Overall, the essays of Frankena, Singer, and Flew concur in the judgment that skepticism is inadequate. Their disagreement, if any, comes with respect to the close connection between morality and rationality. This relation, explicitly asserted by Frankena and at least implied by Singer, has of course the consequence that there are moral obligations for every human being, so that no man can exclude himself from the moral enterprise. Whether a rational morality is possible seems more doubtful in the case of Flew. In refuting Socrates' refutation of

Thrasymachus, he does not of course intend to defend sophistic relativism; but the remark at the end of his essay seems to leave the whole question of the relation between virtue and reason quite ambiguous.

The discussions in this volume do not establish "beyond doubt" the falsity of moral skepticism. But they must certainly force the honest student of morality to question whether skepticism is the best answer, either theoretically or practically, to the perennial question, What is good action and how do I know I am acting morally? Even in an age where (as we have said) ethical relativism is at once so popular and so attractive, the seeker after truth may be moved by the sincerity of the philosophers who appear in this collection to subject the claims of moral subjectivism to the same rigorous critique that the skeptic is presumed, perhaps too optimistically, to have leveled against all forms of moral objectivism. The careful analysis of moral skepticism found in these pages, with its insistence on the necessity of stating the skeptical arguments in all their force as a condition for their refutation, should insure, however paradoxically, that even the skeptic will have a more honest intellectual understanding of his position, its difficulties no less than its advantages, if he will "follow the argument" as it is proposed by our authors.

What positive contribution, then, do these essays make in support of "the moral point of view"? Surely they give evidence that it is *not*, as so many of its opponents have charged, an outmoded or anemic answer to the moral problem. And the flexible moral objectivism that they propose insures that a commitment to moral principles derived from reason is totally compatible with openness to man's evolving knowledge about himself, as well as with sensitivity to the actual phenomena of his moral experience.

NOTES

[1] I am grateful to my colleague William E. Dooley, S.J., for his invaluable criticisms of earlier drafts of this essay; to Mr. Douglas Rasmussen for assistance with research and bibliographical work; and to my wife for her special support, including the typing.

[2] The first and the second of these are suggested in *The Random House Dictionary of the English Language*, ed., Jess Stein (New York: Random House, 1967), p. 1335. The third is a compilation of R. F. Holland's and my own views. See R. F. Holland and Jonathan Harrison, "Moral Skepticism" (Symposium), *Proceedings of the Aristotelian Society*, Suppl. XLI (1967), pp. 185–214.

[3] See Holland and Harrison, p. 200. See also James B. Pritchard, ed., *Ancient Near East Texts* (Princeton: Princeton University Press, 1969).

[4] See Holland and Harrison, p. 200.

[5] Some of these points are suggested in statements of Holland and Harrison, *ibid. et passim.*

[6] D.H. Munro, *Empiricism and Ethics* (Cambridge: The University Press, 1967), ch. 10, defends certain forms of relativism of attitudes in morality which are similar to views criticized here by Singer.

[7] William Frankena, "Recent Conceptions of Morality," in *Morality and the Language of Conduct*, ed., Hector-Neri Castaneda and George Nakhnikian (Detroit: Wayne State Univ. Press, 1965), p. 2. See also "The Concept of Morality," in *The Definition of Morality*, ed., G. Wallace and A.D.M. Walker (London: Methuen, 1970), as well as

in *Readings In Contemporary Ethical Theory*, ed., K. Pahel and M. Schiller (Englewood Cliffs, N.J.: Prentice Hall, 1970); "On Saying the Ethical Thing," *Proceedings and Addresses of the American Philosophical Association*, XXXIX (1966), pp. 21–42; as well as other essays by Frankena where brief mention of "the moral point of view" is made.

[8]Frankena, "Recent Conceptions of Morality."

[9]Frankena, "The Concept of Morality," Pahel and Schiller, p. 391.

[10]See Frankena, "The Concept of Social Justice," in *Social Justice*, ed., Richard Brandt (Englewood Cliffs, N.J.: Prentice-Hall, 1962), p. 26.

[11]Frankena, "On Saying the Ethical Thing," p. 37.

[12]*Ibid.*, p. 40. Disagreement would indicate that the disputants hold different beliefs or have different facts, or else that one or both of them are not acting rationally.

[13]Edvard Westermarck, *Ethical Relativity* (Westport, Conn.: Greenwood, 1970).

[14]A.J. Ayer, *Language, Truth and Logic*, 2nd ed. (London: Victor Gollancz, 1948), p. 108.

[15]Ralph Linton, "Universal Ethical Principles," in *Moral Principles in Action*, ed., Ruth Anshen (New York: Harper, 1952).

[16]R. Firth, "Ethical Absolutism and the Ideal Observer," *Philosophy and Phenomenological Research*, XII (1952), pp. 317–345.

[17]Kurt Baier, *The Moral Point of View*, abridged edition (New York: Random House, 1965), pp. 112–117. See also Baier's "The Point of View of Morality," *Australasian Journal of Philosophy*, XXXII (1954), pp. 104–134.

[18]Baier, *The Moral Point of View*, p. 113.

[19]*Ibid.*, pp. 113–115. True morality so conceived consists of " 'true moral convictions' whose content has nothing to do with social conditions" and which are "based solely on human nature." Except for the claim of its having met certain tests whose nature is unspecified here, Baier's set of true moral principles appears to be subject to the same objections as Frankena raises against Linton. There is an apparent circularity in Baier's notion of true morality, for it turns out that there is no distinction between true morality and the test of morality.

[20]*Ibid.*, p. 115.

[21]Earlier Baier has stated that "our moral convictions are true if they can be required or acceptable from the moral point of view," *ibid.*, pp. 90–91.

[22]Frankena, "The Concept of Morality," in Pahel and Schiller, pp. 394–397.

[23]Other versions of the moral point of view can be found in Paul W. Taylor, *Normative Discourse* (Englewood Cliffs, N.J.: Prentice-Hall, 1961); Kai Nielsen, "Appraising Doing the Thing Done," *Journal of Philosophy*, LVII (1960), 149–159, and "On Moral Truth," in *Studies in Moral Philosophy*, ed., Nicholas Rescher (Oxford: Basil Blackwell, 1968), pp. 9–25; G.J. Warnock, *Contemporary Moral Philosophy* (New York: St. Martin's Press, 1966), ch. 5; and J.O. Urmson, *The Emotive Theory of Ethics* (London: Oxford Univ. Press, 1968), ch. 9. These versions are identified in James Rachels, "Evaluating from a Point of View," *The Journal of Value Inquiry*, VI (1972), pp. 144–157.

[24]Philippa Foot, "In Defence of the Hypothetical Imperative," *Philosophic Exchange*, I (1971), pp. 137–145.

[25]*Ibid.*, p. 143.

[26]*Ibid.*, p. 144.

[27]P. Taylor, pp. 103–124, 294, 295, 304, 305.

[28]See Henry Aiken, "The Concept of Moral Objectivity," *Reason and Conduct* (New York: Knopf, 1962), pp. 134–170; James Rachels, "Evaluating From Point of View," *The Journal of Value Inquiry*, VI (1972), pp. 144–157; J. C. Thornton, "Can the Moral Point of View Be Justified?" *Australasian Journal of Philospohy*, XLII (1964), pp. 22–34; Kai Nielsen, "Anthropology and Ethics," *The Journal of Value Inquiry*, V (1971), pp. 253–266, and "Ethical Relativism and the Facts of Cultural Relativity," *Social Research* XXXIII (1966), pp. 531–551.

[29]Aiken, pp. 138, 139, 161.

[30]Rachels, pp. 144–157.

[31]*Ibid.*, p. 151.

[32]Taylor, pp. 108, 109.

[33]William Frankena, *Ethics* (Englewood, Cliffs, N.J.: Prentice-Hall, 1963), pp. 37–42.

[34]A fuller examination of the details of Rachels' arguments is warranted, but it cannot be done here. However, examination of its details would strengthen rather than qualify the reservations expressed above.

[35]Nielsen, "Anthropology and Ethics," p. 253.

[36]Clyde Kluckhohn, "Ethical Relativity: Sic et Non," *Journal of Philosophy*, LII (1955), pp. 663–677.

[37]Nielsen, p. 253.

[38]*Ibid.*, p. 261.

[39]Taylor, p. 108. Implicit in Frankena's account of the moral point of view is its cross-cultural character.

[40]Marcus G. Singer, *Generalization in Ethics* (New York: Knopf, 1961), pp. 327–334.

[41]These descriptions are based on those given below by Singer.

[42]For other studies on personal subjectivism see George Roberts, "Some Refutations of Private Subjectivism in Ethics," *The Journal of Value Inquiry*, V (1971), pp. 292–309; Paul Edwards, *The Logic of Moral Discourse* (New York: Free Press, 1955), ch. 2.

[43]Ayer, ch. 6; C. L. Stevenson, *Ethics and Language* (New Haven: Yale Univ. Press, 1944).

[44]Singer, *Generalization in Ethics*.

[45]Monro, pp. 117–123.

[46]*Ibid.*, p. 122.

[47]Singer, *Generalization in Ethics*, esp. pp. 327 ff.

[48]G. E. Moore, *Principia Ethica* (Cambridge: The University Press, 1903).

[49]For some recent studies of Thrasymachus' thesis and the problem of morality and reward see Philippa Foot, "Moral Beliefs," *Proceedings of the Aristotelian Society*, LIX (1958–59), pp. 83–104; D. Z. Phillips, "Does It Pay to Be Good?" *Proceedings of the Aristotelian Society*, LXV (1964–65), pp. 45–60; Peter Wertheim, "Morality and Advantage," *Australasian Journal of Philosophy*, XLII (1964), pp. 375–387; Peter Winch, "Can a Good Man Be Harmed?" *Proceedings of the Aristotelian Society*, LXVI (1965–66), pp. 55–70; L. Wittgenstein, *The Notebooks: 1914–1916* (London: Kegan Paul, 1914–1916).

[50]I am especially indebted to the helpful comments of Professor William Dooley, S.J. on the Socrate-Thrasymachus debate.

THE PRINCIPLES OF MORALITY
WILLIAM FRANKENA

We often speak of morality as a human or social enterprise or institution more or less coordinate with art, education, law, and science—for example, when we ask how morality is related to law or to religion, or when we talk about the moral sphere as contrasted with the legal or scientific ones. Here "morality" is used not as the opposite of "immorality" but rather to refer to the moral as distinct from what is nonmoral or pertains to other areas of human interest. This is what R. B. Perry had in mind when he said, ". . . there is something which goes on in the world to which it is appropriate to give the name of 'morality.' Nothing is more familiar; nothing is more obscure in its meaning."[1]

Even when we think of morality in this way, however, we use expressions of two rather different kinds. On the one hand, we use expressions like:

> "the morality of the Chinese,"
> "ancient morality,"
> "the new morality,"
> "business morality,"
> "his morality,"
> "a moral code."

In such phrases "morality" seems to refer to something that is relative to an individual, group, or period, something that is variable and changeable. On the other hand, we also use phrases such as:

"the moral law,"
"the moral ideal,"
"the morally good man,"
"the morally right way to act,"
"what morality requires,"
"the supreme principle of morality,"
"the principles (dictates, precepts,
        rules, demands, etc.) of morality."

In these uses "morality" and its cognates appear to refer to something that is not relative and variable, something that is somehow absolute and unchanging—to something like what Ralph Cudworth called "eternal and immutable morality." These expressions imply or presuppose, not only that morality is an enterprise distinct from the others mentioned earlier, with its own ideals, principles, or requirements, but also that it is an enterprise in which only one ideal or principle, or one set of ideals or principles, is recognized as valid. Thus, on the one hand, we speak as if there are or could be many moralities or moral action-guides, and, on the other, as if there is or can be only one.

This distinction between what we may call "relative" and "absolute" uses of "moral" and "morality" has been somewhat neglected in our pluralistically and relativistically-minded culture, even by moral philosophers.[2] But there it is—and no account of morality that ignores it, or fails to give an analysis of both kinds of expressions, can be regarded as complete.

The need for recognizing the difference between these two kinds of expressions and senses of "morality" can be illustrated by a sentence from P. W. Taylor: " . . . morality is a set of social rules and standards that guide the conduct of people in a culture."[3] This is what *a* morality or moral code is —it is a set of standards that guide the conduct of an individual or group. But "morality" as it is used in phrases of the second sort is, so I shall argue, not just a set of standards actually followed, but something more like the true set of standards.

In some earlier papers I dealt with the problem of defining morality in the sense in which it is something relative and variable—that is, I tried to say something about the criteria for distinguishing moralities from other things like religions, legal systems, etc., or for distinguishing moral action-guides from non-moral (as distinct from immoral) ones.[4] In this essay I shall pay attention to expressions in the second group, seeking to show what they mean and to defend their use, partly because their use is not entirely clear, and partly because it is constantly under attack in the century in which we live. Sometimes our culture and especially its sub-cultures seem to be opposed to morality in *any* form, but, in any case, though we continue to use the phrases in question, we seem on all sides to be against recognizing it in any *absolute* form.

I

Let us see then what we do or should take expressions in our second group to mean. I shall first state and consider four views about this and then propose and defend a fifth. Then in continuing my defense of this fifth view I shall present and discuss two more. Finally I shall conclude by commenting on an eighth position.

(1) To a "contemporary" who has gotten "with it," it is tempting to say the following: in the expressions of our second group we mean by "morality" and "moral requirements," the prevailing and generally accepted ideals, rules, etc., of our culture or society (i.e. those that belong to *our* moral action-guide), and, when we say, "The principles of morality are . . . "or "Morality requires . . . ," all we mean is "Our society demands . . . " or "The moral code of our culture includes . . . ," or something of this sort. Students find this view hanging in the air about them like a smog, and breathe it in—and out —as if it were healthy. It appears to be almost taken for granted in psychology and the social sciences. Philosophers, who ought to know better, sometimes also take it for granted. It is the sort of view Bertrand Russell summed up in the remark, "Conscience is the still small voice that tells you someone else is looking."

I submit, however, that this is not, need not be, and should not be what we mean when we use the expressions in question.[5] When one says firsthand that P is a principle of morality, he is himself espousing, and should be understood as espousing, P as part of his own moral action-guide; he is not just saying that it is part of the prevailing moral code— unless he is in effect using "morality" in quotation marks and gives us some indication that he is doing so.

Perhaps, in order to allow for this "inverted comma" way of speaking, we should distinguish between two ways of using the phrases under discussion.[6] There is an "external," spectator way of speaking, which is used when a psychologist or sociologist says, "The requirements of morality are just internalized parental rules." A legal scientist may make statements about what the law is in a similar sense, without subscribing to the law he is stating. Or, suppose that one of our "uncommitted" ones says, as he tramples on them, "So much for the dictates of morality!" He is not just a spectator or scientist then, of course, but he *is* an outsider of a kind who does not subscribe to what he calls "the dictates of morality," though his society does. There is, however, also an "internal," subscribing way of speaking, "prescriptive" in Hare's sense of prescribing to oneself as well as to others, which I take to be the normal one. Here the speaker assents to what he calls "the principles of morality" or just "morality," at least in his preaching, if not in his practice. He takes the moral point of view; he is not an outsider, a spectator, a scientist, a skeptic, or an "alienated" man—as our first theory implies that he is.

Returning to the consideration of this theory, it should be observed that it does not allow for the possibility of criticizing a prevailing morality on

moral grounds, something we often do and presumably desire to go on doing. If by "the principles
of morality" we mean only "the principles of our
prevailing morality," then we cannot even suggest,
let alone proclaim, that there are moral principles
that ought to be recognized in our culture but are
not. We can charge our morality with being unclear
or inconsistent, and we can accuse ourselves of not
living up to it, but we cannot claim to have found
any new moral principles or ideals. We also cannot
condemn on moral grounds the moral code of
another culture; we can only say that its principles
are different from ours.

(2) The next "contemporary" move, of course, is
to say: "Oh, that's right! When one says 'P is a
principle of morality' or 'Morality dictates . . . ,' he
does not ordinarily mean merely that others take it
to be part of their moral action-guides. He is expressing his own moral convictions. What he means to
say is not 'My *culture* demands . . . ,' but rather, '*My*
moral code requires . . . '; not 'Someone else is looking,' but 'I am looking.' More simply, he is saying
'*I* approve of . . . '—that and nothing more is what
he means." This view of the matter is also mistaken.
When one says "P is a principle of morality," one
does not merely *assert* the *fact* that he subscribes to P
or approves of action in accordance with P, or the
fact that his own moral code includes P. He is actually approving or subscribing in his very statement: his utterance is "performative" in J. L.
Austin's sense.[7] And this means, as I see it, among
other things, that he is claiming in his utterance that

acting on P and approving of such action are in some way justified or rational. That is, when one says, "It is a requirement of morality that . . . ," he is not just saying, "The prevailing morality requires that . . . ," *or* "My morality requires that . . . ," *or even*, "The morality I regard as valid requires that . . . ," *but* something like "True morality requires that . . . ." This last statement may be construed as just a fancy way of saying, "We are morally required to . . . ," but then *this* does not mean simply "It is a rule of prevailing morality that . . . ," or "It is a rule in my moral code that . . . ," or "On what I regard as moral grounds I favor . . . ."

(3) A third and more sophisticated contemporary doctrine would reply as follows at this point: "Of course, when one says 'Morality requires . . . ,' 'The morally good man does . . . ,' or 'I approve of . . . ,' one is not merely *asserting that* something is the case about oneself, one's moral code, or that of one's society. One does not mean simply *that* one or one's society is in favor of something or regards it as the thing to do; rather, one is *taking* and *expressing* a pro-attitude toward a certain kind of character or conduct. But, either *that* is all one is doing or should be taken as doing, or one is doing that and also trying to evoke a similar pro-attitude in others—and *that* is all he is doing."[8]

The main point to be made in reply to this third view is similar to the one made a moment ago in dealing with the second contemporary move, namely, that when one says, "Morality requires . . . ," one is not merely venting one's emotions or pro-attitudes or trying to arouse similar ones in others. In W. D. Falk's term,[9] one is "guiding," not "goading" or commanding, oneself or others. Certainly one is not simply "expressing" oneself. One is claiming that some action, attitude, disposition, or way of life is justified or rational at least from the moral point of view.[10] One *is* having and expressing a moral sentiment about something, but one is not merely expressing it and seeking to evoke it in others. Rather, one is assuming it in oneself and others and then judging, from this point of view, that some action or way of life or quality of character is desirable, justified, or rational. And, in using in the ordinary way the expressions we are studying, one is subscribing to a certain action-guide and claiming that it is the "true" one from the moral point of view. Once again, "Morality requires . . . " means something like "True morality, which I hereby subscribe to and urge you to subscribe to, requires . . . ," where saying "True morality requires . . ." is not just a way of emphasizing one's pro-attitude or reinforcing one's goading of others, as is "Big Brother is watching you."

Here I must comment on the phrase "true morality," which I have used once or twice and which appears every now and then even in this "postmodern" age. It is an ambiguous expression and may have at least the following three meanings. (a) It may mean "true virtue," "true moral goodness," or "the truly right way to live." Then it refers to what is truly moral as opposed to immoral. In this sense, "True morality requires . . . " says

much the same thing as "We have a moral obligation to do . . . ." The main difference is that it makes
more explicit the claim that moral codes which do
not require the conduct in question are mistaken (a
claim also made by the latter utterance but only
implicitly).[11] That is why the use of "true" here is
not merely an endorsing or emphasizing use or even
a "persuasive" one. (b) It may, for example, in "a
true morality," be used to refer to any action-guide
that meets the "true" requirements for being a *moral*
action-guide. Here it stands for what is truly moral
as opposed to non-moral, not for what is truly moral
as opposed to immoral. For example, P. F. Strawson
seems to use "true morality" to mean any socially
accepted action-guide that satisfies the ordinary concept of morality.[12] (c) It may also mean, or be taken
to mean, "the action-guide that both passes the
tests for being a moral (as versus non-moral) action-
guide *and* the tests for being true, justified, rational,
or valid from the moral point of view." This is the
sense in which I am using "true morality," and I
believe it is what Kurt Baier means by "absolute
morality."[13]

It follows from what was said in (1), (2), and (3)
that "P is a principle of morality" does not mean
"P is a principle in the code that I (and/or my
society) take to be important, overriding, or
supreme."[14]

(4) There is a fourth interpretation of expressions
like "The principles of morality" and "Morality requires . . ." about which I ought to say a word. An
anthropologist like Ralph Linton might argue that

all accepted moral action-guides include certain
prohibitions or requirements, e.g. not to kill a fellow-
tribesman or citizen except in self-defense, and that
"morality," in the phrases we are concerned with,
should be taken to mean the totality of these universally accepted norms.[15] This interpretation has
some advantages over the previous three—it gives
our phrases a more objectivistic meaning, as is required—but it will not do all that is wanted. It does
not permit us to say that the principles on which all
prevailing social moralities agree are not really the
principles of morality. It tells us, in effect, that to
find out what the principles of morality are we must
and need only see what norms are actually accepted
by all cultures. But what we mean—and want to
mean—when we speak of "the requirements of morality," etc., is not the totality of universally prevailing norms, whatever these are, but rather, to quote
a Dutch dictionary definition of the moral law
(*zedewet*), "*het geheel van de normen die het zedelijk leven
moeten beheersen*" (the totality of the norms that should
govern the moral life)—or, as I would prefer to put
it, the totality of rationally justified moral norms,
the action-guide that both fulfills the criteria for
being a moral action-guide *and* is rationally most
justifiable from the moral point of view.

II

(5) Thus I arrive at a fifth view, which has been
adumbrated in what has been said, and which I
shall now try to clarify and defend. An analogy with

enterprises other than morality may help here. I wish to maintain that the expressions "moral requirements," "the principles of morality," etc., are like "science tells us . . . ," "history teaches us . . . ," "the laws of nature," etc. When one says "history tells us" or "science tells us" something, let us say P, then one is subscribing to P, but one is also taking, or purporting to take, the historical or scientific point of view, and claiming that P is true or rationally justified by the evidence from that point of view —or as W. P. Alston might put it, one is "taking responsibility for" its being rationally justified from that point of view.[16] In other words, one is subscribing to P from a certain point of view and claiming that everyone who views the evidence carefully from that point of view will eventually also subscribe to P. Notice here how different "history tells us" is from "historians tell us," and "science tells us" from "scientists tell us." Now I suggest that "morality tells us" is like "history tells us" and "science tells us" in this respect—and not like "moralists tell us," "society tells us," etc. When one says "P is a principle of morality" one is taking or purporting to take the moral point of view, subscribing to P from that point of view, and claiming that P is rationally justified by the facts as seen from that point of view or that everyone who views the facts carefully from that point of view will eventually also subscribe to P.

A point about this fifth view needs clearing up. Roughly, I am holding that when a person says "Morality requires P," he means by "morality" true morality in the sense of "the action-guide that ful-

fills the criteria for being a moral one and is rationally justified from the moral point of view," or "the
moral action-guide to which all those who are fully
rational within the moral point of view will eventually agree." And he is in some way implying that
he is both taking the moral point of view and subscribing to P. He is, however, not saying or implying
that he actually subscribes to the true morality,
since he may not know what this is (he claims that
P belongs to it, but he does not now know that it
does). Yet he is not speaking as an outsider or spectator either, one who is not subscribing to any moral
action-guide but only to some belief or fact about
himself or the society around him. He subscribes to
true morality in intent or promise, just as in doing
science one subscribes in intent or promise to the
findings of science, whatever they turn out to be, or
much as Socrates subscribed to the "laws" of Athens,
whatever they might turn out to be, by the mere
fact of his remaining there. In this sense, "the principles of morality" are something to be *discovered* (or
possibly "revealed"), not something to be created,
invented, or decided on by a sheer act of "decision"
or "commitment" on one's own part, as so many
seem to think nowadays. Thus I reject the notion
that when one refers to "the principles of morality"
one is simply referring to principles that one accepts
as basic or proposes to adopt by some kind of fiat,
though I do want to say that when one uses such
phrases one *is* then and there subscribing to the
principles one refers to.

　　Suppose, then, that I ask the question, "What are

the principles of morality?", and set out to find the answer. The answer is not to look to see what P's are accepted by me, my society, or everyone, or to make any sheer decisions, however anxious, authentic, or profound, or even to look around for some Ideal Observers or gods and see what P's they accept. It is to take a certain (the moral) point of view myself as fully and "coolly" as I can, get myself clear-headed, logically rigorous, and fully informed about relevant facts, and see what I cannot but accept under those conditions, much as I do when I ask and try to discover the principles of bookcase-building or the laws of nature and of nature's science. Even then the principles I accept (or "decide on") may not *be* "the principles of morality" but I will justifiably claim that they are and call them by that name.

Thus, in such expressions as "the principles of morality," "morality requires," and "the moral ideal," what is ordinarily referred to may be defined as that moral action-guide which, in Baier's words, "can be seen to be required or acceptable *from the moral point of view*"[17]—or, more fully, as the moral action-guide that everyone who looks at the world clear-headedly and informedly from that point of view will eventually agree on.[18] When one makes a moral judgment, espouses a moral ideal, proposes a moral code, etc., one subscribes to it as required from the moral point of view or claims that it is or is included in or entailed by "true morality" in the sense indicated above. In short, our moral discourse, especially in such expressions as I have been con-

cerned with, involves the concept of an objectively
or absolutely valid moral action-guide, and our
moral judgments and decisions claim to be parts or
applications of such an action-guide. Moreover, I
maintain that we may and should go on thinking
and speaking in this way.

III

In reply to this fifth view, which I am advocating,
an opponent may take at least three lines of attack.

(a) He may contend that there is no such thing as
the moral point of view in any worthwhile sense—
that there is an irreducible plurality of moral points
of view such that there will also be an irreducible
plurality of "true moralities" or of action-guides
that can be seen to be required or acceptable from
some genuinely moral point of view, with no rational way of choosing between them (except, perhaps, from some non-moral point of view). Part of
the time, it looks as if H. D. Aiken means to mount
this line of attack.[19] I am not convinced that it is
anything like fatal to my position, but cannot discuss it here.

(b) He may argue that, while there is such a thing
as *the* moral point of view (as is claimed in every
firsthand moral judgment), it is not true that everyone who takes that point of view and is rational
within it will eventually find the same action-guide
to be required or acceptable. Not all disagreements
in attitude or action-guidance, he may say, are
rooted in differences in factual belief, concept for-

mation, or logic. Hence we ought to give up claiming any kind of rational or interpersonal justifiability or validity for our moral judgments and decisions, and eschew all talk of a true or absolutely valid morality—or, if we keep the talk for its "emotive" force, we should at least give up the idea that has gone with it. To this line of thought I can only say here that, though one cannot prove its premises to be mistaken, neither can its proponent prove them to be correct, and that I therefore choose to stay with the objectivism I take to be involved in our ordinary concept of morality. More generally, I see nothing in these two lines of attack that requires us to give up our absolutist ways of speaking or thinking, no conclusive reasons for accepting a proposal that we revise our moral thought and expression in a more relativistic or pluralistic direction.

(c) But, in his essay, "The Concept of Moral Objectivity,"[20] Aiken advances a third line of thought that seems calculated, partly to show that the ordinary moral discourse we have been reviewing does not actually involve any such absolutism or objectivism as I have been describing, and partly to convince us that, even if it does, we ought to be brave, new, and mature enough to give it up. This line of thought is what I mainly want to discuss in the rest of this paper, in defense of my view as stated earlier.

IV

Before I do so, however, it will be useful to discuss

a sixth view of the expressions we are concerned
with—that of Roderick Firth[21]—together with
Aiken's critique of this view.[22] On Firth's view, when
I say "Morality requires . . . ," "The principles of
morality are . . . ," etc., I am saying or mean that
the conduct or principles in question are or will be
approved by an Ideal Observer who is omniscient,
omnipercipient, disinterested, dispassionate, and
consistent. Against this position, Aiken has two
arguments, both in essence familiar: (a) the open
question argument, and (b) the argument that "disinterestedness," etc., cannot be defined "without
reference to principles antecedently acknowledged
as moral." Now, I am by no means convinced that
these arguments come off, and, indeed, I still agree
with Firth that, when I say "Morality requires . . ."
or make any moral judgment, I am claiming that
any Ideal Observer would agree, though I worry
about some of the details of his definition of an Ideal
Observer, as R. B. Brandt and others have.[23] But I
agree with Aiken in thinking that Firth's view—a
form of ethical naturalism—cannot be accepted without qualification. For, as I see it, when I say "Morality requires . . . ," etc., I am not merely *asserting*
that an Ideal Observer, however he or it may be
defined, does or will or would approve or agree. I
am not that purely cognitive or spectatorial; I am,
as I said before, speaking as an insider, I am taking
a pro-attitude myself, I am myself subscribing or
approving at least in intention or promise—in short,
I am trying to *be* an Ideal Observer taking the moral
point of view and I am approving or disapproving

on the basis of what I then see. As was intimated earlier, I am not simply looking around at Ideal Observers to see if any or all of them agree, though I am claiming they will if there are any, and I profess a readiness to revise what I say if they do not. I also agree with Aiken to the extent of holding that any Ideal Observer appealed to must be taking a point of view antecedently acknowledged as moral, and I am not sure he is doing this simply in being disinterested, dispassionate, and consistent. Thus there is a good deal of force in Aiken's arguments against Firth; they do show Firth's view to be inadequate. But I do not see that they show more than this, or that all forms of absolutism are mistaken— and I shall try to explain why.

V

Aiken's "bearings in moral philosophy," new or old, are in many ways much like mine. In particular, he would, I think, agree with my criticisms of the four views discussed and rejected earlier, except for the absolutism broached in them. At any rate, he also rejects those views. However, he resolutely refuses to accept anything like the fifth view I have been advocating, either as a descriptive-elucidatory thesis about our actual moral discourse and reasoning or as a normative proposal about them. He also adopts a more pluralistic position about the moral point of view: "There can be," he says flatly, "no such thing as 'the moral point of view' . . . ."[24] Thus he, in effect, provides us with a seventh view of the meaning of the expressions under investigation.

I cannot deal adequately with all of Aiken's complex but interesting and stimulating paper. For present purposes, the main point is that he offers us a non-absolutistic, quasi-existentialist conception of the objectivity claimed in moral judgments. It is non-descriptivist or non-cognitivistic, like mine, but, while it provides moral judgments with a *kind* of objectivity, as mine does, it denies them even the rather Peircean *claim* to being absolute that I take to be implied in them. Yet Aiken insists that his conception is faithful to "the ordinary notion of moral objectivity." I shall maintain that it is not. It will be necessary here to quote at some length.

In [the workaday] world the problem of moral objectivity is mainly a problem of piecemeal mutual adjustment of acknowledged commitments within a loose framework of precepts and practices, none of which is ever permanently earmarked as an absolutely first principle and each of which is subject to a list of exceptions that can never be exhaustively stated. . . .

What is wanted is not a better understanding of the hypothetical reactions of a perfectly objective somebody-else, but that conscientious second thought which enables us to take a more general view of our own existing responsibilities. Such a general view provides no definition of moral right and wrong; it does not require us to ignore "our own" when we find that their claims upon us cannot conscientiously be universalized; it does not demand that we treat "everybody," whoever they may be, as moral persons; nor does it commit us to some supposed consensus of moral opinion which all other "competent" moral agents must be presumed to share. In brief, there is and can be no absolute or universal vantage point from which conscientious moralists, regardless of their sentiments, may make an objective appraisal of their particular moral decision and principles. Morally, we are always in the middle of things, confronted with eternally exceptionable precepts which, until such exceptions have been made, still lay presumptive claims upon us that we cannot in conscience disavow. What provides the basis for such exceptions? Nothing save other particular principles which, in turn, we are forever driven to qualify in the light of still other principles. And when we come temporarily to the end of a line of qualifications what do we find? To our dismay, nothing but the very "first-level" duties with which we began.

The ordinary principle of moral objectivity thus prescribes, not that we look beyond the moral life itself for a ground of criticism, but only that we search within it for the soberest and steadiest judgment of which, in the light of all relevant obligations, we are capable. When a question arises concerning the objectivity of a particular moral judgment or principle, our task is always and only to look beyond *it* to the

other relevant commitments which we ourselves
acknowledge. And if this answer seems inadequate, then the reply must be that there is, in
conscience, nothing else to go on. In the moral
sphere it is always, finally, up to us; nor is there
anyone to whose steadier shoulders our burden
of moral judgment can be shifted. That is the
agony of the moral life; it is also its peculiar
glory.

The only principle of objectivity in morals is,
then, essentially a principle of reconsideration.
What it demands, when a question about the
objectivity of a particular judgment or principle
arises, is that we consider whether such a judgment or principle, as it stands, can be consistently upheld in the face of whatever other
moral considerations might be thought, in conscience, to defeat it. . . .

In summary, there is and can be no definitive
criterion of moral objectivity and, hence, no
definitive principle of moral right and wrong.
When a serious question about the objectivity
of a particular moral judgment or principle
arises, there is simply the further *moral* obligation to re-examine it in the light of the other
obligations and duties that have a bearing upon
it. If it should be replied that objective reconsideration requires, also, an endless search for
new facts which, if known, might alter our
notions of our obligations and duties themselves, the answer must be that such a search
would defeat the very purpose of moral reflec-

tion, which is *judgment*. The principle of objectivity requires only that we take account of any hitherto unconsidered facts to which we may reasonably be expected to have access. But in that case what is reasonable? There is no formula for answering such a question; our judgment can be formed only by weighing the obligation to look for relevant facts against other obligations. In a word, the principle of moral objectivity can neither supply the materials for moral judgment nor tell us where to go in search of them. If we have no time to search for further possibly relevant facts, the principle of objectivity will provide us with not one moment more; if we are otherwise lacking in moral sensibility, it will not make good our deficiency by so much as a single obligation. What it can do—and it can do no more—is to dispose us to review our decisions so that we may neglect no pertinent fact that, in the time we have, is available to us and that we may neglect no obligation which deserves to be considered. Primarily, therefore, it functions as a principle of falsification, and what consistently survives the general scrutiny which it demands may pass as objectively valid or true.[25]

There is a great deal in these and in the supporting paragraphs that one must agree with. I am ready to agree that it is in general correct as a description (phenomenological?) of what we *do* when we are trying to solve a moral problem or reach a moral conclusion either about a particular case or about a general principle—even the bit about the agony and the ecstasy of the moral life. What then is there in what Aiken writes here that a would-be absolutist of my kind cannot accept? It is not "the principle of reconsideration," which Aiken says is "the only principle of objectivity in morals." The necessity and possibility of reconsideration is precisely what I regard as recognized in the claim of a moral judgment that it will hold up through any further reconsideration. If Aiken is saying anything I must disagree with, as he certainly means to be doing, it must be the following two things.

(a) One is the contention that we do *not* in fact claim in our moral judgments—not even when we use expressions of the second sort listed at the beginning—that they will be sustained by *all* further reconsideration of them (and of any principles they involve) in the light of "possibly relevant facts." This contention seems to be implied when Aiken writes that the objectivity called for in "the world of workaday moral problems and judgments" does not "commit us to some supposed consensus of moral opinion which all other 'competent' moral agents must be supposed to share."

(b) The other is the thesis that we claim *only* that our moral judgments will hold up through a certain kind of rather limited reconsideration—that, while we do claim a certain objective validity for our moral judgments, it is only a limited one with no absolutism whatsoever in it. It should be noted here that, if Aiken is saying only that all we ever do in our moral deliberations is to go through a limited and not an "endless" reconsideration, he is, of course, right. But any absolutist can admit this. After all, life is short and *tempus* does *fugit*. Again, if he is asserting only that it is sometimes reasonable and right to cut off our search for possibly relevant facts and to come to a moral "judgment," then he is right too. But, once more, no absolutist denies this; admitting it is quite compatible with holding that when we do come to make the judgment, we are claiming that it will be sustained by all possible reconsideration and not merely that it is the best we can do or reasonably be expected to do under the circumstances. Therefore, Aiken must be asserting (b). And, since (b) entails (a), we may concentrate on (b). What, then, is the limited kind of reconsideration that he regards as necessary and sufficient in morals?

Aiken describes it as follows in the paragraphs quoted: (1) as "a piecemeal mutual adjustment of acknowledged commitments within a loose framework of precepts and practices, none of which is ever permanently earmarked as an absolutely first principle and each of which is subject to a list of exceptions that can never be exhaustively stated"; (2) as a "search . . . for the soberest and steadiest judgment of which, in the light of all relevant obligations [and facts?], we are capable . . . , our task [being] always and only to look beyond *it* to the other relevant commitments which we ourselves acknowledge"; (3) as considering "whether [our] judgment or principle, as it stands, can be consis-

tently upheld in the face of whatever other moral
considerations might be thought, in conscience, to
defeat it"; (4) as taking facts into account as well as
moral principles, but only such facts as "we may
reasonably be expected to have access" to in the
time available to us.

As I said, I believe that these descriptions add up
to a very good account of all that we do or can be
required to do in deciding moral questions—except
that I would like to bring in the business of taking
"the moral point of view," especially when it comes
to reconsidering our moral principles (and Aiken
comes close to doing this when he says "relevant"
and "in conscience"). What bothers me here is the
fact that Aiken is by implication reducing the *claim*
of moral judgments to objectivity to a claim that
they will be upheld by a reconsideration in the light
of moral principles one acknowledges to oneself, and
of such facts as one may reasonably be expected to
have access to. What, it may be asked, is wrong with
doing this? The trouble is that there is an ambiguity.
Aiken must, it seems to me, assert one of two things:
(1) that, when I make a moral judgment, I am
claiming only that it is or would be upheld by a
careful review of the matter in the light of the moral
principles I *already* acknowledge, and of the facts
that I can reasonably be expected to have access to
at or *before* the moment of judging, or (2) that, when
I make a moral judgment, I am claiming that it is
or will be upheld by a careful review of the matter
in the light of the moral principles I *may come* to
acknowledge "in conscience" and of the facts I *may*

come to have access to and be reasonably expected to make use of in such a review.

Suppose that Aiken affirms the former, as his anti-absolutism suggests he must. Then I have three comments. (a) What he says strikes me as false—just as false as if one were to say the parallel thing about the making of factual judgments. It seems, especially, to be inadequate as an account of what we are to do when we reconsider our moral principles themselves—it does not even provide for the possibility of doing this. (b) Suppose that I did not make my moral judgment or decision carelessly—that before I made it, I did in fact make a careful review of the matter in the light of all the principles I then acknowledged, and of all the facts I could then reasonably be expected to pay attention to. Then my claim to objective validity would be impeccable; I could in no sense say on the next day, if I came to acknowledge other principles and have access to further facts, that my judgment was mistaken. I could, if Aiken's view is that represented by (1), only change my mind, and would need to feel no anxiety about this, existential or otherwise. (c) According to (1), in reconsidering my judgment or decision the next day, I need (and may) only rethink the matter in the light of the principles I acknowledged *the day before* and of the facts I could *then* reasonably have been expected to consider. This is possible, but it seems clearly not to be what we should do when we are really reconsidering.

Suppose, on the other hand, that Aiken subscribes to (2), as he seems to when he writes that "the principle of objectivity may require reconsideration of any judgment [or principle?]." Then he is coming very close to the kind of absolutism about the objectivity claimed by a moral judgment that I have advocated. It may be that he would (in the interest of "autonomy") underline the "I's" in the formulation of (2), so as not to bring in any claim to a possible consensus with *others*. But then I am not sure there really is a difference between us, especially if the individual making a moral judgment is not assumed to be in some special position with regard to the facts or particularly susceptible to certain kinds of principles, for then he can always be replaced by others. If, however, he is assumed to be peculiar or in some unique position, then, again, I think that (2) is plainly false—that Hume (who is not unadmired by Aiken) had things right when he said that in making a moral judgment I choose a point of view common to myself and others and express sentiments in which I expect all my audience are to concur with me.

At this point, Aiken would probably contend that there is no such thing as *the* moral point of view, so that there must always remain an irreducible pluralism in the moral enterprise. He does say this at least twice.[26] This contention is, however, not established by the discussion we are reviewing, and, as I have already intimated, Aiken seems to recognize something like the moral point of view when he speaks of "conscience" and "moral commitments."

In this connection Aiken makes some play with the open question argument.[27] (a) It looks as if he would use it against all attempts to define the moral point of view and the distinction between moral and non-moral action-guides. That is, he would insist that one can say of any point of view or action-guide, "Yes, it fulfills your criteria, but is it moral?" And, of course, one can, if by "moral" one means the opposite of "immoral." To allege, however, that one can always say it when one clear-headedly means by "moral" the opposite of "non-moral" is to beg the question, which is precisely whether the definition is satisfactory or not.[28]

(b) More to the point here is the fact that it appears as if Aiken would also use a kind of open question argument against all kinds of absolutism, and not only against that of Firth. Then, against me, for example, he would have to argue that one can always say of something, "Yes, it would be approved by all those who are fully rational within the moral point of view, but is it morally right (or good)?" or, "X might be approved by all those who are fully rational from the moral point of view and yet not be morally right (or good)." My reply comes in two parts. First, I grant that one can agree that X is or would be approved by all who are fully rational within the moral point of view and not agree that it is morally right or good. For one might be what I earlier called an outsider or spectator and not be ready to make any moral judgment whatsoever. As I said before, when one says "Morality requires . . ." or makes any moral judgment, one is not merely asserting that it is or would be agreed to by all who are fully rational from the moral point of view; one is oneself taking that point of view and judging from it. But, secondly, if anyone is to get mileage out of the open question argument at this point, he must claim that an *insider* who speaks from the moral point of view or "in conscience" can sensibly ask the open question. And this I doubt. An insider could say, "X may be approved by all . . . and yet *be* wrong or bad." But can he sensibly say that it would be approved by *anyone* who . . . , and then *himself* go on to *judge* that it is not right or good? Perhaps he can if he is himself not clear-headed or fully cognizant of relevant facts or not taking the moral point of view (as he claims to be), though I am not sure that he could in that case know that X is or would be approved by those who take the moral point of view, are clear-headed, etc. Suppose, however, that he is himself fully cognizant of relevant facts, etc., and actually taking the moral point of view. Then, surely, there *is* at least a "pragmatic paradox" in his saying that X would be approved by all who . . . , and then going on to disapprove of it. For then his own moral judgment constitutes an exception to the statement he has just made and presumably has not yet forgotten.

It does not appear, then, that an open question argument is fatal to the form of absolutism I have advanced, and we may conclude that we both do give and may go on giving an absolutist sense of the kind indicated to such expressions as "the principles of morality" or "morality requires . . . ," and, for that matter, to all our firsthand moral judgments. *Should* we continue to do so? One could at this point reply simply by asking, "Why not?" But, it is worth suggesting that it may be man is fully human only insofar as he asserts in himself "the image of God," as people used to call it, and bravely claims for his enterprises—science, history, art, and morality— some kind of final and rational validity.

VI

There is an eighth position about which something may now be said against the above background, namely, the view that "the moral law," etc., refer to the commands of God. This position makes "the principles of morality" stand for something that is or is claimed to be absolute, and so is like the fifth and sixth positions discussed above (mine and Firth's), and opposed to the others, including Aiken's. But it may take either an intellectualistic or a voluntaristic form, depending on its answer to the question, "Is P commanded by God because it is a principle of morality or is it a principle of morality because it is commanded by God?" If it gives the first answer, we may interpret it as holding that God commands what he commands because he takes the moral point of view and is fully rational within it (clear-headed, fully informed, etc.). Then it is essentially a form of either the fifth or the sixth of the above positions and stands or falls with them. If it answers that P is a principle of morality simply because it is commanded by God, then and only then does it really constitute an eighth position—one that is absolutistic and yet conceives of the principles of morality as being ultimately (not for us but for God) matters of arbitrary choice or decision. God might then have made not-P a principle of morality simply by deciding to; his choice between P and not-P would not be dictated by his nature, by his reason, or by anything whatsoever. No claim would be made that he is taking the moral point of view or that his choice will be sustained by the consideration of rational beings. When I say "P is a principle of morality" I would be claiming that God wills that we act on P, but not that P will be agreed to eventually by all who take the moral point of view and are rational within it.

Now, I doubt that, when we say, "P is a principle of morality," we *mean* only that P is commanded by God. For, once more, when we say this, we are also indicating that we ourselves accept P as a part of our own moral action-guide (perhaps *because* we believe it to be commanded by God). This point, of course, can be accepted by the theological voluntarist with only a slight emendation of his position. It also still seems to me, however, that, when we accept P as a principle of morality, we are claiming more than simply that it is commanded by God. For (a) we do most naturally give the intellectualistic answer to the above question, as is shown by Socrates' conversation with Euthyphro; (b) if we give it up, this is not on the basis of a study of moral concepts or discourse, but on the basis of theological considerations; and (c) we really believe that God commands P (as a "moral" principle, as distinct from a "positive" duty like keeping the sacraments) only if we believe that P is rational or justifiable from the moral point of view. Or else we have a sense of utter paradox, as we do if we take seriously the case of Abraham's being commanded by God to sacrifice Isaac. In fact, I suggest that what makes the equation of the principles of morality with the law of God plausible is precisely an implicit assumption that God *is* fully rational and *does* take the moral point of view. With this assumption it makes perfectly good sense to say that the principles of morality are those that would be sustained by the judgment of God, and even an atheist may agree.[29]

VII

There is a poem by Wallace Stevens that I cannot refrain from mentioning in conclusion. It is entitled "Sketch of the Ultimate Politician," but, with what precedes in mind, I could wish it had been called "Sketch of the Ultimate Moralist."

He is the final builder of the total building,
The final dreamer of the total dream,
Or will be. Building and dream are one.

There is a total building and there is
A total dream. There are words of this,
Words, in a storm, that beat around the shapes.

There is a storm much like the crying of the wind.
Words that come out of us like words within,
That have rankled for many lives and made no
    sound.

He can hear them, like people on the walls,
Running in the rises of common speech,
Crying as that speech falls as if to fail.

There is a building stands in a ruinous storm,
A dream interrupted out of the past,
From beside us, from where we have yet to live.

If I am right, then we are all would-be ultimate
moralists, whether we know it or not, when we use
expressions like "the principles of morality." For
then there is a total building of which we are all
dreaming. And there are words of this that come out
of us and beat about the shapes and run in the rises
of common speech—words like "the requirements
of morality," "the right thing to do," and "the
moral ideal." These words have rankled for many
lives and made no sound, but today, when that
speech falls as if to fail in the ruinous storm of our
time (the new morality, God-is-dead-ism, and all
that), they remain like people on the walls crying
to us from where we have yet to live.

NOTES:

[1]*Realms of Value* (Cambridge: Harvard University Press, 1954),
p. 86.

[2]For an exposition of the distinction, see J. Kemp, *Reason, Action and
Morality* (New York: Humanities Press, 1964), pp. 183 ff. It is half
recognized by J. H. Hartland-Swann, *An Analysis of Morals* (London:
Allen and Unwin, 1960), pp. 62–67. Recognition of it would also
have helped Kurt Baier's discussion in *The Moral Point of View*, rev.
ed. (Ithaca, New York: Cornell Univ. Press, 1965), pp. 82 ff. Among
other things, it is important to recognize that one may agree that a

certain code or principle is a moral one in the "relative" sense and deny that it is one in the "absolute" sense.

[3]*Problems in Moral Philosophy* (Encino, Calif.: Dickenson Publ., 1967), p. 8.

[4]See "Recent Conceptions of Morality," *Morality and the Language of Conduct*, ed. H. Castaneda and G. Nakhnikian (Detroit: Wayne State Univ. Press, 1963); "The Concept of Morality," two versions, one reprinted in G. Wallace and A. D. M. Walker, eds., *The Definition of Morality* (London: Methuen, 1970) and the other in K. Pahel and M. Schiller, eds., *Readings in Contemporary Ethical Theory* (Englewood Cliffs, N.J.: Prentice-Hall, 1970). See also "MacIntyre on Defining Morality," reprinted in Wallace and Walker.

[5]Cf. R. F. Atkinson, *Conduct: An Introduction to Moral Philosophy* (London: Macmillan, 1969), pp. 52 f.

[6]Cf. H. L. A. Hart, *The Concept of Law* (Oxford: The Clarendon Press, 1961), pp. 55 f., 86 f., 99; J. D. Urmson, *The Emotive Theory of Ethics* (Phoenix, Ariz.: Hutchinson, 1968), pp. 107 f.

[7]Cf. Urmson, pp. 52 ff., on "I approve of . . . ."

[8]Cf. A. J. Ayer, *Language, Truth and Logic* (London: Victor Gollancz, 1936), ch. VI; C. L. Stevenson, *Ethics and Language* (New Haven: Yale Univ. Press, 1944). For criticism see, e.g., Urmson.

[9]"Goading and Guiding," reprinted in R. Ekman, ed., *Readings in the Problems of Ethics* (New York: Scribner, 1965).

[10]Cf. C. Wellman, *The Language of Ethics* (Cambridge: Harvard Univ. Press, 1961), pp. 258 ff., 263 ff.; Urmson, pp. 56, 58, 63.

[11]Cf. Wellman.

[12]"Social Morality and Individual Ideal," reprinted in I. Ramsey, ed., *Christian Ethics and Contemporary Philosophy* (New York: Macmillan, 1966), pp. 284 ff.

[13]Baier, pp. 112 ff. What he here means by "true morality" is somewhat different, something more like "true morality" in sense (b). Note: *here* Baier comes close to recognizing the distinction between "relative" and "absolute" senses of "morality."

[14]See Hartland-Swann, p. 62.

[15]Cf. Linton, "Universal Ethical Principles," in R. Anshen, ed., *Moral Principles* (New York: Harper, 1952); C. S. Lewis, *The Abolition of Man* (New York: Macmillan, 1947).

[16]*Philosophy of Langague* (Englewood Cliffs, N. J.: Prentice-Hall 1964) p 41.

[17]Baier, pp. 90 ff.

[18]It is in this sense that I take myself to be asserting that the principles of benevolence and justice are the basic principles of morality, in *Ethics* (Englewood Cliffs, N. J.: Prentice-Hall, 1963), pp. 35–42. Cf. pp. 95 f.

[19]See article to be cited in next note.

[20]In *Reason and Conduct* (New York: Knopf, 1962); reprinted in Castaneda and Nakhnikian (subsequent references are to this edition).

[21]Cf. "Ethical Absolutism and the Ideal Observer," *Philosophy and Phenomenological Research*, XIII (1952).

[22]Aiken, pp. 87–94.

[23]Cf. Brandt, "The Definition of an 'Ideal Observer' Theory in Ethics," *Philosophy and Phenomenological Research*, XV (1955), 407–423, with subsequent reply by Firth and rejoinder by Brandt.

[24]Aiken, pp. 74, 79, 95.

[25]*Ibid.*, pp. 96–100.

[26]See note 24.

[27]*Ibid.*, pp. 80, 85. I take the open question argument to be constantly in Aiken's mind in this essay.

[28]Aiken does recognize the difference between the two opposites of "moral" in one reference to the open question, p. 81. But if his "autonomist" can use this point, so can an "objectivist" like myself.

[29]In this connection, cf. R. L. Mouw, "The Status of God's Moral Judgements," *Canadian Journal of Theology*, XVI (1970), pp. 61–66.

MORAL SKEPTICISM[1]
Marcus G. Singer

My topic in this essay is moral skepticism. This is, to be sure, a topic that is rather well worn, but nevertheless I believe that I have something fresh to say on it. Of course, some of the arguments that I shall use were originated or first suggested by others, and I am no longer sure in every case just who these others are. Moreover, even if I am wrong, and if nothing that I have to say is new, at least I may hope that what I have to say is true—and, as William James once said, "Any fool can be original." But, whether well-worn or not, the topic is one of perennial interest and probably ineradicable importance. There is a famous remark of T. H. Green that has been paraphrased as follows: "One is sometimes tempted, indeed, to say that moral philosophy is necessary chiefly to remedy the evils it has itself brought into being."[2] Perhaps this can be taken as something like a motto for our topic.

So much in the way of prelude and apologia; now I shall begin, by presenting a general characterization of moral skepticism.

I

I say a general characterization, and not a definition, because the term "definition" carries an aura
of precision that is not practicable in connection
with this topic. For this is no single or unitary topic.
R. F. Holland, in a fairly recent paper, "Moral
Scepticism," says: "We are without, and so far as
I can see *necessarily* without, any clear idea of what
moral scepticism as an intellectual position amounts
to."[3] This is, I think, much too strong, and perhaps
the difficulty is caused by the fact that there is no
single or unitary intellectual position or theory or
point of view that can appropriately be labeled
"moral skepticism." Moral skepticism comes in many
varieties, though perhaps not the full fifty-seven of
the Heinz Pickle Company. In general, any theory
that maintains that there can be no such thing as a
good reason for a moral judgment, or that there are
no valid moral arguments, or that ultimate moral
principles cannot be proved, that morality has no
rational basis, or that the difference between right
and wrong is merely a matter of taste, opinion, feeling, or convention, is a form of moral skepticism. It
is evident that considerations applicable to one of
these forms may be altogether inapplicable to another.

Perhaps "moral agnosticism" would be a better
name for the type of position, or the attitude, we
shall be considering, or at least certain forms of it.
The term "agnosticism" has come to acquire asso-
ciations with theology that might prejudice its use
in this connection. But insofar as "agnosticism"
denies the possibility of attaining knowledge, truth,

or certainty in a certain area, "moral agnosticism" is an excellent name for the view that we cannot attain moral knowledge, moral truth, or moral certainty—in short, that ultimate moral principles cannot be proved. I am not going to attempt to criticize or refute moral agnosticism here and now. The best way to refute moral agnosticism, if that is what one wants to do, is actually to prove some ultimate moral principle. This is, of course, notoriously difficult. Moreover, if any of the other varieties of moral skepticism is true, it is impossible. If there are no valid moral arguments, if the difference between right and wrong is merely a matter of opinion, custom, or attitude, there can be no proof of an ultimate moral principle. So what one has presented as a proof is bound to be defective, and will almost certainly not be accepted as a proof, as long as other varieties of moral skepticism remain undiscussed. They will haunt those who ignore them, and must be exorcised.

One way of exorcising them is to name them, for to name them is to distinguish them, and if they remain undifferentiated they remain as a vague, brooding presence. So I shall go on to distinguish from one another some varieties of moral skepticism.

II

There are five varieties of moral skepticism that I shall distinguish, though I shall not attempt to discuss them all: (1) Moral Subjectivism; (2) The Emotive Theory; (3) Ethical Relativism; (4) Egoism;

and (5) Determinism or Fatalism. I shall give a brief characterization of each of these.

(1) *Moral Subjectivism* maintains that moral or value judgments are statements to the effect that the speaker, or someone else, has a certain attitude, usually characterized as that of approval or disapproval, toward the action, practice, or person referred to.

There are actually two forms of this view, which I shall call *Personal Subjectivism* and *Social Subjectivism*.

According to personal subjectivism, to say that something "is right" or "is good" is to say that I, the speaker, approve of it. To say "*X* is wrong" (or "*X* is bad") is to say that I, the speaker, disapprove of *X*.

According to social subjectivism, to say that something is right or good is to say that people generally, or the majority of one's own society, approve of it, whereas to say that something is wrong or bad is to say that people generally, or the majority of one's own society, disapprove of it.

It is pretty clear why this type of view should be called Subjectivism. Even though on this view moral judgments are allowed to be true or false, and even a variety of factual statements—since it is a plain matter of fact whether a person or a group approves or disapproves of something—yet this fact is about the person or group in question, and not primarily about the action or whatever it is that is referred to in the statement of the judgment. Thus, on this view, moral judgments are statements of subjective facts.

(2) The emotive theory, as it has come to be called, can be traced back to David Hume's *Treatise of Human Nature*, which appeared in 1740. In this century it has received its most striking and forceful formulation in A. J. Ayer's *Language, Truth and Logic*, and it is primarily in Ayer's formulation that I shall consider it, though I shall later make references to other forms of it.

On this view moral or value judgments are not interpreted as statements at all. That is, they are not interpreted as statements that are capable of being true or false, not even as statements to the effect that someone or other has a certain feeling or attitude. They are, rather, interpreted as *expressions* of feeling or emotion. It is part of this view that moral or ethical or value terms have no literal or descriptive meaning (they do not serve to describe, do not attribute properties), and therefore must be interpreted as having only emotive force or "emotive meaning," that is, as merely expressing certain feelings or emotions on the part of the user. Thus, to quote Mr. Ayer: "In every case in which one would commonly be said to be making an ethical judgment, the function of the relevant ethical word is purely 'emotive.' It is used to express feeling about certain objects, but not to make any assertion about them."[4]

It is easy to see how the views so far mentioned are forms of moral skepticism, as I have characterized it, and it is in fact these two (or three) views, or varieties of skepticism, that I shall actually discuss.

(3) *Ethical Relativism*. This term, in the wider

sense, is often used as equivalent to moral skepticism generally. In the narrower sense, this term is associated with the fact that moral beliefs and standards vary from place to place and from time to time, which gives rise to the idea that they are all "relative" to place and time. Ethical relativism is the theory that all moral ideas are necessarily "relative to" a particular society, in the sense that they reflect the "standpoint" of some particular society and only "hold for" that society, so that in case of a conflict between these different standards there is no way of impartially or objectively or rationally deciding between them; any reason that might be given would itself merely reflect the standpoint of the group to which one belongs. Thus on this theory all moral judgments are incomplete unless they specify "the standpoint" from which they are made, and it is a further consequence of it that moral judgments are really expressions of the attitude or characteristic bias of a particular group. On this view, in other words, there is nothing that can correctly be said to be right or wrong; it is only a question of what is *called* "right" or "wrong," and by what group it is so called.

This theory is to be distinguished from *moral* (or *cultural*) *diversity*, which is the *fact* that there are a great many different and even conflicting rules and practices prevailing at different times and in different places, so that what is regarded as right in one place may be regarded as wrong in another. Ethical relativism is not a fact, but a theory, which attempts to account for this fact of moral diversity.

Whether it does so, and how well it does so, are philosophical questions of some import.

(4) *Egoism.* Here I refer to Psychological Egoism, the view that everyone is actuated by self-interest; that whenever anyone acts, he acts in order to benefit himself, regardless of the effects of his action upon others, except in so far as these effects must be taken account of in ensuring one's own benefit. This view does not really fall under the characterization I gave earlier of moral skepticism. It is a *source* of moral skepticism, rather than a *form* of it, as can be seen from the fact that, if it were true, it would follow that moral arguments and moral standards would be pointless, since they could never influence conduct. It is also connected with skepticism through the fact that it is one of the sources of the perennial question, "Why should I be moral?"—as though the objectivity of moral ideas depended on their capacity to elicit universal agreement both in belief and conduct.

(5) Finally, *Determinism* or *Fatalism.* I am speaking of Determinism in the sense in which it maintains that whatever anyone does is caused by factors over which he has no control, so that whatever anyone does, he could not have acted any differently by any conscious effort. It should be clear how, like Egoism, Determinism in the sense specified is a source of, or leads to, moral skepticism, since it would destroy the point of moral ideas. In fact, Egoism itself is simply a form of this sort of Determinism. I am aware of the fact that Determinism can be formulated in such a way as not to lead to

these consequences. With these other formulations of it I am not now concerned. However, I shall not discuss this view further except to say that I am not aware of any form of this view that I find either persuasive or plausible. The view, and certain of the facts that lead to it, however, do raise important questions for practical ethics.

III

So much for preliminaries. Let us now consider personal subjectivism.

Both forms of subjectivism are advanced as analyses of moral or value judgments, of the meaning of moral or ethical terms. They are responses to the apparent difficulty of settling moral questions and resolving moral disputes. But there is really, as we shall see, very little to be said for either of them. So I shall simply present some criticisms of each. The value is in the criticisms, and in considering them we may get a little better understanding of what we mean when we say that something is right or wrong.

A. According to personal subjectivism, let us recall, a moral or value judgment is an assertion to the effect that the speaker has a certain attitude, either favorable or unfavorable, toward the action or person or thing the speaker is ostensibly judging.

First, on this view, what sense could be made of a moral *question?* The question, "Is *X* right?", or "Ought *X* to be done?", would mean "Do I approve of *X*?", or "Do I disapprove of not doing *X*?" I do not recognize this as a question that anyone has ever wanted to ask, as distinct from the question "*Should* I approve of X?", a question that cannot, on this view, be given a sensible interpretation. (It would mean: "Do I approve of approving of X?", or else, "Do I disapprove of not approving of X?") One can say, "I am not sure whether I approve of X or not." This is *not* equivalent to asking, "Do I approve of X?" After all, whom is one asking? Moreover, presumably the one asking such a question does not antecedently approve of X, so that his answer to the question "Do I approve of X?" would have to be, "No." This would mean that he disapproves of it, so he must regard X as wrong. But a similar situation holds if he asks "Do I disapprove of X?" His answer must be "No" (otherwise he would not have the original question). This would mean that he must regard X as right, but this contradicts the original hypothesis. I can see only confusion here. One way out for the subjectivist is to say that in such a case the person in question neither approves nor disapproves of X. That means that he must regard X as morally indifferent. But then what would have been the point in the original question? Again, it is simply absurd to suppose that one who cannot make up his mind whether he approves or disapproves of an action must regard it as morally indifferent; this was not his view in originally asking the question. Finally, this view can provide no guidance whatever *toward answering* the question "Is X right?" No doubt a defender of the view would admit this; but it is still worth pointing out.

Second, on this view, it is difficult to see how

moral disagreements or arguments could be possible. For, on this view, if A says "X is right," and B says, "X is wrong," they are not disagreeing, because they are not contradicting each other.[5] Both remarks are consistent with one another. In order to express his disagreement with A, B would have to say "No, you don't!" Apart from the fact that it is dubious that this is what B was originally talking about (namely, A's attitude toward X), as a statement about how we do in fact express or indicate moral disagreements it is blatantly false, and as a recommendation as to how we should express or formulate such disagreements it is blatantly absurd. Moreover, it seems very dubious that a person could with any frequency be *mistaken* about his own attitudes, and even more dubious that another person should be better acquainted with them in practically every case in which moral disagreement is expressed; in the way in which, according to this view, disagreement should be expressed, one would have to accuse the other party to the dispute of *lying* about his own attitudes.

Third, the definition of "right" and "wrong" in terms of approval and disapproval is nonsensical, since it can never finally be stated. To approve of something is to regard it as right; to disapprove of something is to regard it as wrong. To regard an act as right is to think that it is right; to regard it as wrong is to think that it is wrong. Consequently, "That act is right" means "I approve of that act," which means "I regard that act as right," which means "I think that act is right," which means "I think I think that act is right," which means "I think I think I think that act is right," and so on, indefinitely and frivolously. This is then the view that anyone who makes a moral judgment must be stuttering.

The upshot is this. There is a difference in import between asserting "*X* is right" and asserting "I approve of *X*"; it is the difference between the more confident and the less confident assertion of the judgment that *X* is right. From the fact that someone asserts "*X* is right" it can be inferred, if his assertion is honest, that he approves of *X*, that is, that he regards *X* as right. But this holds for any assertion—from the fact that it is made one can infer, on the assumption that it is honestly made, that the speaker believes what he is saying.

I conclude that there is good reason for not accepting personal subjectivism as an account of the nature or meaning of moral judgments.

B. Let us recall that social subjectivism is the view that to assert that something is right or wrong, or good or bad, is to assert that society approves of it or disapproves of it, and the latter is intended as an analysis of the former. This view has been widely attributed to Hume. That it is an accurate representation of Hume's view is very dubious. It does not follow, however, that no one has ever held it. We can find it in a widely used psychology text:

To behave morally is to behave in the way that society approves. When a person obeys the rules and laws of his society, we say he is *moral*

or good; when he disobeys, we say he is immoral or bad. We must draw another distinction to cover the individual who because of low
intelligence or unfamiliarity with the code
sometimes violates it. Such a person is called
amoral (lacking in morals) and is not classed as
either good or bad.[6]

This view has considerable appeal, and many people
find it very plausible. I think this may be because it
has not been clearly understood. So let us consider
it.

(1) If this view were true, then no one could
morally criticize his own community, or the majority view on some matter, without either contradicting himself or uttering nonsense. For let us
suppose that people generally, or the majority of
people in one's community, approve of, say, segregation. On this view, this means that segregation is
right. If now one were to say that segregation is
wrong, he would be saying that people generally,
or the majority of people in his community, disapprove of segregation. To say that society is wrong
in sanctioning or approving of segregation would be
to say that society both approves and disapproves of
segregation, and this is self-contradictory, or else it
is to say that society disapproves of its approving of
segregation, which is surely nonsense. The upshot
is that on this view it is impossible to criticize the
standards of one's own society without contradicting
oneself or making a senseless statement. Think of
any law or institution or practice of your society

that you regard as morally objectionable, and on this view you are thinking something that cannot be thought. I don't think anyone can think this. Any such criticism can of course be mistaken or unfounded, but it is simply absurd to say that it *must* be, because it must be self-contradictory or senseless.

(2) On this view, no sense could be made of a moral question or perplexity, except as a question about what the majority opinion is, which could be settled by collecting statistics, or by public opinion surveys, and this is absurd.[7] Such a view would make Dr. Gallup, or Lou Harris, or even Dr. Kinsey, the moral experts of our time. Who can believe this?

(3) Let us suppose that this theory became known to the majority of people, and that they came to accept it as an adequate account of the meaning of the concepts of "right" and "wrong." Then no one could have any view on whether some kind of act was right or wrong unless he knew what the majority attitude on the matter was. But since this applies to each, it applies to all, with the consequence that the community, or the majority, could have no attitude toward it. With each person waiting for the others to make up their minds or form an attitude, and the others waiting for each other, no result could be arrived at. Then we would truly have a "great silent majority."

These points, taken together, indicate pretty decisively that social subjectivism cannot be maintained. What, then, explains the strong appeal it has for people? I think what happens is that people are taken with the idea that society exercises a conditioning or an indoctrinating effect on individuals, so that most people's attitudes on most things are determined by their cultural milieu. Certain basic institutions, such as the school, certainly have as one of their main aims that of inducing a basic conformity on values the society regards as most vital to its continued existence. From this idea of the way in which we acquire our moral beliefs and attitudes, it seems like an easy move to the philosophical theory that this is all that we mean by them. But this is a mistake. There can be little doubt of the existence and the importance of this conditioning effect. But there can be doubts about its value, and this by itself should indicate that the empirical facts just mentioned cannot be evidence for the philosophical theory of social subjectivism.

C. In this connection it is worth considering briefly a view I did not mention previously, which I shall call the *Social Pressure Theory of Obligation*. This is the view that what is called "obligation" is just a feeling of compulsion, resulting from social pressure, or the desire to conform. In other words, if I claim or feel that I have an obligation to do something, this so-called "obligation" is merely a feeling of compulsion on my part to do it, resulting from the pressures exerted on me to do it by society. However, this theory is incapable of distinguishing the "compulsion" characteristic of an obligation from any other sort of compulsion. The hand-washing compulsion, or the compulsion to avoid stepping on the lines in a sidewalk, is never, or hardly ever, felt by anyone as an obligation. Moreover, this theory can make no sense of other than first-person obligation statements. If I say "You ought . . . ," or "You have an obligation . . . ," I am surely not saying that you feel under a compulsion to do the thing in question. For one thing, if you were to deny that you felt any such compulsion, I should not for a moment take this as invalidating my statement. For another, this theory would make such a statement as "You have an obligation to overcome your compulsion to do X" self-contradictory, which it most assuredly is not. Similar points apply to third-person obligation statements.

IV

The *Emotive Theory of Ethics* (or *Values*) developed out of a consideration of the consequences of just such criticisms of subjectivism as the ones I have presented. It was intended to be an improvement on them and to overcome the objections that seemed to be most telling against the various forms of subjectivism. So the emotive theory is more interesting, and certainly more sophisticated, but, in my opinion, no closer to the truth.

A. First some remarks, of a general character, some of which are applicable both to the emotive theory and to subjectivism.

These theories are best interpreted as *hypotheses* intended to account for certain facts about morality. The reason for this interpretation is that one can find no positive evidence anywhere for them, in the sense of deductive arguments, premises from which the theory or analysis is deduced. The theory is simply asserted, in the hope that its assertion and elaboration and application to various examples will prove sufficiently convincing. To quote Mr. Ayer again:

> We shall meet the difficulty by showing that the correct treatment of ethical statements is afforded by a third theory, which is wholly compatible with our radical empiricism.
>
> We begin by admitting that the fundamental ethical concepts are unanalysable, inasmuch as there is no criterion by which one can test the validity of the judgements in which they occur. So far we are in agreement with the absolutists. But, unlike the absolutists, we are able to give an explanation of this fact about ethical concepts. We say that the reason why they are unanalysable is that they are mere pseudo-concepts. The presence of an ethical symbol in a proposition adds nothing to its factual content. Thus if I say to someone, "You acted wrongly in stealing that money," I am not stating anything more than if I had simply said, "You stole that money." In adding that this action is wrong I am not making any further statement about it. I am simply evincing my moral disapproval of it. It is as if I had simply said, "You stole that money," in a peculiar tone of horror, or written it with the addition of some special exclamation marks. The tone, or the exclamation mark, adds noth-

ing to the literal meaning of the sentence. It
merely serves to show that the expression of it
is attended by certain feelings in the speaker.[8]

Notice that there is no argument here whatsoever;
there is simply asseveration. Ayer says he is going to
show that the correct treatment of ethical statements
is afforded by his theory, but he *shows* nothing of the
sort. His statement, "We *say* that the reason why
they are unanalysable is that they are mere pseudo-
concepts" is, in this respect, much more accurate.
Notice also his claim to be able to "give an explanation of this fact about ethical concepts"—the fact, or
alleged fact, that they are "unanalysable." It is at
this point that one fundamental question is begged.
For Ayer says that he admits that "the fundamental
ethical concepts are unanalysable, *inasmuch as there
is no criterion by which one can test the validity of the
judgements in which they occur.*" This is simply to
assume moral agnosticism. He has not shown, or
even argued, that there is no such criterion. (In
fact, no one has shown this.) He simply takes this
fundamental point for granted. (It is interesting to
note, incidentally, that Ayer's *criterion* for saying that
"the fundamental ethical concepts are *unanalysable*"
is that there is no criterion for testing the validity of
the judgments in which they occur. On this account,
since it is not proved that there is no criterion for
testing validity, it is not proved that these concepts
"are unanalysable.") Another point at which a fundamental question is begged is in the assertion that
in claiming that an action is wrong I am simply

evincing my *moral* disapproval of it. What is meant
by moral disapproval, as distinguished from disapproval of other kinds, is left unexplained. It ought
also to be explained how disapproval differs from
disliking: someone can disapprove of something
without disliking it.

Now I have not quoted and commented on this
passage in order to make debater's points. There is
nothing wrong in a theory's being advanced as a
hypothesis, intended to account for certain facts.
This may well be the best way to proceed in moral
philosophy. Yet this point raises some basic questions, which will provide us with a point of view
from which to examine this theory.

If the theory is advanced as a hypothesis, we are
entitled to ask just what the evidence for it is. I
suggest that we consider the theory, in the first
place, in the light of the following four questions:

(1) What facts is it intended to account for?

(2) Are these alleged facts really facts?

(3) Could any other theory just as readily account
for these facts, insofar as they are facts?

(4) Are there any facts about morality that it
does not account for? (We should remember once
more that some of these points are applicable to
Subjectivism, as well as to the Emotive Theory.)

Well, what are some of the facts, or alleged facts,
about morality the theory is intended to account
for? I shall mention and discuss four.

(1) The first is the fact of perpetual and widespread disagreement about morality. Under this
heading is supposed to be accommodated the fact

that there is apparently irreconcilable disagreement and dispute about what is right and what is wrong, about what is good and what is bad, and about whether something ought or ought not to have been done. But this fact is exaggerated. There is no more widespread disagreement about morality than there is about questions of many other kinds: philosophical questions, questions about the past, about who started an argument, and so on. Moreover, this fact can be explained on other grounds—as a result of ignorance, misinterpretation, faulty reasoning, and misapplication of moral rules, to mention some. So it provides no unequivocal support for the theory.

(2) The second fact, or alleged fact, is the fact of widespread disagreement on the theoretical level, the level of ethical theory: the fact that no ethical theory has yet attained anything approximating universal or even widespread acceptance, and that there seems very little chance that any will. The emotive theory, if true, would explain this fact, on the ground that there is actually nothing to agree on. This point, however, really proves nothing, and is actually self-refuting. Since the emotive theory itself has not attained widespread acceptance, on this line of reasoning it must be rejected. (It would thus amount to saying: "Moral judgments, bah!")

(3) Thirdly, there is the fact that we resort to abuse in moral or value disputes. As Ayer puts it: "It is because argument fails us when we come to deal with pure questions of value, as distinct from questions of fact, that we finally resort to mere abuse."[9]

But, in the first place, this is not peculiar to disputes about values or morals, and, in the second place, it is not common to all of them. Moral questions are not the only ones about which disagreements arise, and moral disputes are not the only ones that lead to heated and abusive words, or even to blows. People get abusive in arguing about such simple and trivial matters of fact as the batting average of some baseball player or the physical dimensions of some movie star. But neither is it *characteristic* of moral disputes that they lead to abusive words. It all depends on the character of the persons who are arguing. Some people get abusive in any kind of dispute, especially if they feel it is going against them. Some people never, or hardly ever, do. To generalize about the character of moral disputes from partial observations of the behavior of uneducated roughnecks or people with emotional disturbances seems to me decidedly unphilosophical.

So this "fact" is only an alleged one. And there is no call for a theory to explain what isn't so.

(4) Fourthly, there is the argument, representing a fact, that "it is possible for two people to agree on all the facts of a case, and yet disagree in their evaluations or moral judgments about it." This is a claim that one often hears made, and it is supposed to follow from this that moral judgments or evaluations are subjective or emotive or incitive-emotive, and so on. But this does not follow at all. It is true that people can *in fact* do this, that such disagreements can occur (though only within limits, because it is not possible to be certain that *all* the facts

of a case have actually been specified). But this proves nothing. What has to be shown is that neither party to the dispute is being unreasonable or irrational in so disagreeing, and this does not follow from the mere fact of disagreement. It is possible for two people to agree on the truth of the premises of a simple syllogism, and still disagree on what conclusion follows from them. For it is possible for people to be irrational, or to commit errors in reasoning. If this is possible with a simple syllogism, as it is, it is certainly possible with more complicated deductive arguments. Consider, for example, the inference: "There are more trees in the world than there are leaves on any one tree, and there are no trees with no leaves at all; therefore there must be at least two trees with the same number of leaves." In any group of people not consisting solely of professional mathematicians the question whether the conclusion follows will generate considerable disagreement. That it can readily be shown to follow is irrelevant. Disagreement has been shown to be possible. Again, it is possible for two people to agree about the facts of the present international situation, and to disagree about its outcome, what will happen next. It does not follow that predictions of the future are therefore subjective, or emotive, or expressive of attitudes. The fact that such disagreements can occur, therefore, is no evidence for the subjective or emotive character of moral judgments or evaluations.

So, considered as a hypothesis, the theory falls short. It assumes certain things to be facts about morality that are not really facts, it does not account for the facts that it does account for more readily or plausibly than other theories can, and there are facts about morality it does not and cannot account for.

In connection with the point just made (and a point made earlier in connection with subjectivism —namely, if the theory were true, how would moral disputes be possible?), Ayer presents an especially interesting and perplexing argument, which is worth some consideration. He denies that anyone ever really does dispute about questions of value. He says: "We certainly do engage in disputes which are ordinarily regarded as disputes about questions of value. But, in all such cases, we find, if we consider the matter closely, that the dispute is not really about a question of value, but about a question of fact."[10] He admits that "this may seem, at first sight, to be a very paradoxical assertion." I believe that it is more paradoxical than he supposes. For, apart from the fact that genuine arguments about moral matters occur—which cannot be reduced to arguments "about a question of logic or about an empirical matter of fact"—if genuine disputes about value or moral questions were actually impossible, as Ayer claims, then he would have no way of identifying instances of arguments which he claims cannot possibly occur. (Moral questions certainly depend on determinations of fact—though it is not clear how this theory can account for this—but that is not all they depend upon.)

B. At this point I should like to consider an aspect of the emotive theory that I have so far not mentioned, its analysis of moral judgments as involving

imperatives or disguised commands.[11] According
to Ayer:

> Ethical terms do not serve only to express
> feeling. They are calculated also to arouse feel-
> ing, and so to stimulate action. Indeed some of
> them are used in such a way as to give the
> sentences in which they occur the effect of
> commands. Thus the sentence "It is your duty
> to tell the truth" may be regarded both as the
> expression of a certain sort of ethical feeling
> [notice again this unexplained reference to
> ethical feeling] about truthfulness and as the
> expression of the command "Tell the truth."
> The sentence "You ought to tell the truth"
> also involves the command "Tell the truth",
> but here the tone of the command is less em-
> phatic. In the sentence "It is good to tell the
> truth" the command has become little more
> than a suggestion . . . .[12]

I shall only mention two obvious, and, in my opinion, conclusive objections to this account. The analysis of moral judgments, or ought statements, as
imperatives or commands, is clearly inapplicable to
other than second-person ought statements, and to
moral judgments made about actions that have
occurred in the past. "Brutus ought not to have
taken part in the assassination of Caesar" cannot
with any shred of plausibility be interpreted as a
command. But this view is clearly wrong on other
grounds as well. Try translating "I am not sure, but

I think you ought to do X," into a command. It cannot be done. Advice cannot be transformed into a command, even by the magic of linguistic analysis.

C. Now for some more direct criticisms of the emotive theory proper.

(1) There are logical relationships, such as contradiction and entailment, between ethical statements, or the statements of moral judgments. But there can be no such relationships between expressions of emotion, or between emotions themselves. For example, "A has the duty to do X" contradicts "A has the right not to do X," and "A has the duty to do X" entails (and is entailed by) "A has no right not to do X." But it does not even make sense to speak of an expression of emotion, such as "Ugh!" contradicting, entailing, or being consistent with "Sigh!", "Ouch!", or "Hurry!" It follows from this that, although the statement of a moral judgment may serve to express the emotions of the speaker (it is a generally overlooked fact that practically any statement can serve to express emotion), moral judgments cannot be *mere* expressions of emotion. But this is what the emotive theory asserts them to be.

(2) Again, it is a fact that reasons can be given for moral judgments, and that we can distinguish between considerations that are morally relevant and those that are morally irrelevant. For example, the color of one's eyes is ordinarily irrelevant to a moral judgment about one's actions or one's character (though in certain very unusual circumstances such a consideration might be relevant). This is a

fact that is perfectly obvious (and there are hosts of similar examples that could be given), and I might add that it is more obvious and certain than the emotive analysis itself. How does this weigh against the emotive theory? Very simply. On this theory such facts would not be possible. For it is not possible to give (justifying) reasons for or against mere expressions of emotion, and it makes no sense to speak of considerations that are relevant or irrelevant to them.

(3) I am not implying that it is always obvious whether a consideration is morally relevant or irrelevant. I have said only that it is sometimes obvious. But it is one of the tasks of an ethical theory to provide criteria for determining the moral relevance of certain kinds of considerations. This brings me to my next criticism of this theory. *It is morally irrelevant.* And it is morally irrelevant because it has no relevance whatsoever to moral problems and perplexities about what ought to be done. These problems remain, even for one who adopts this theory as an analysis of the nature or meaning of moral judgments. Thus this theory can be no substitute for a theory that does have such relevance. (This point, incidentally, applies also to Subjectivism.)

D. I have so far said nothing about a consideration that is probably the main source of the emotive theory (though by itself it does not support this theory rather than some form of subjectivism): the so-called principle of verifiability, which maintains (roughly) that a statement has literal meaning or significance if and only if it is either logically certifiable or verifiable by sense experience. One reason I have said nothing about it is lack of space. Another is the conviction that it is not really necessary. If the criticisms I have made so far are sound, there is no real need to consider this principle; and the criticisms I have made so far derive from ethics, not epistemology. I might add, however, that one difficulty with the principle is that "literal significance" has not been defined independently of it, which makes it circular. Another is that there is no good reason to accept it.

V

Another matter about which I have said nothing is the analysis of moral judgments presented by C. L. Stevenson, and this is an omission that should be rectified. There can be no doubt that Stevenson's form of the emotive theory (as he himself calls it) has been the most influential among contemporary philosophers. There is also no doubt that his analysis is subtle, sophisticated, persuasive, and considerably elusive. Stevenson takes as his main subject of examination such statements as "This is good" (and does not think that there are any significant differences between this and other forms of evaluative or normative statements). He analyzes this statement as meaning: "I approve of this: do so as well." (It is true that he says this is only a characterization of its meaning, not a definition, but he operates with it as though it were a definition, and so I shall do the same.)

Stevenson says of this account that it contains two elements: "First a declarative statement, 'I approve' or 'I disapprove,' which describes the attitudes of the speaker, and secondly an imperative statement, 'do so as well,' which is addressed to changing or intensifying the attitudes of the hearer."[13] Now I find it tempting to say that a chain is no stronger than its weakest link, and that Stevenson's analysis consists of two links, "I approve of this," and "Do so as well," neither of which has the strength required of it. However, although some of the criticisms I have already made of the analysis of moral judgments as statements of approval or disapproval will apply to Stevenson's analysis, not all of them will. Moreover, the imperative component of the analysis is said to be intended to modify the attitudes of the hearer, rather than as a direct command to him to act in a certain way, so what I have already said of the imperative analysis of moral judgments will here be inapplicable. So the analogy of a chain, tempting as it is to use it, will not here apply. And Stevenson says, quite rightly I think, that "these components, acting together, readily provide for agreement or disagreement in attitude," though I think that this begs the question whether agreement and disagreement in *attitude* is what is important or even relevant in connection with moral judgments and disagreements.

Let us consider what sense this analysis can make of a moral question such as "Is X good?", or "Is X right?" It has always struck me as strange that Stevenson begins one of his most famous papers on

this subject with the remark: "Ethical questions first
arise in the form 'Is so and so good?' or 'Is this alternative better than that?',"[14] and then proceeds to
say practically nothing further about the analysis
of ethical questions; in particular, he fails to apply
his analysis of ethical assertions back to the analysis
of such ethical questions. What does "Is X good?"
mean on Stevenson's analysis? In fact, what can it
mean? He analyzes it (or so he told me directly) as
meaning: "Do I approve of this? Are others to do so
as well?" I must confess that I regard this as ludi-
crous, though it may very well be a logical consequence of the theory. I have already considered the
question "Do I approve of this?" and rejected it as
an inadequate analysis of an ethical question. I see
no need to take seriously the other component of
the analysis, "Are others to do so as well?", for I do
not regard it as making any sense whatsoever. How
would one go about answering it? The most it can
mean is "*Should* others do so as well?", but this leaves
us where we started, for it contains the word
"should," which must presumably be eliminated in
favor of some reference to attitudes.

In actual print, Stevenson has another, different
account of the meaning of ethical questions. He says:
" 'Is X good?' is a remark that prompts an ethical
judgment from the hearer, and can readily be taken
to mean, 'Do *you* approve of X, and shall I?' The
phrase, 'Shall I?' is a request for influence, and can
roughly be compared to a request to be commanded,
as in the context, 'Shall I take the left turn, or the
right?' "[15] But it is simply false that to ask whether

something is good is "to ask for *influence*," as Stevenson claims.[16] If I were to ask *myself* this question, how would I go about influencing myself? I am surely not asking myself to influence myself, nor am I requesting myself to command myself. If you go pretty fast in the wrong direction, you can go pretty far wrong, and that, it seems to me, is what Mr. Stevenson has done here. So there is good reason for not accepting this analysis.

Finally (and this point applies equally to the other analyses I have considered), let us consider what would happen if an analysis like Stevenson's were to become universally known and universally accepted. If all I meant to say, when I said that something was right or good, was that "I approve of it; do so as well," and if this were all anyone meant to say and all anyone understood anyone else to mean by it, it is impossible to suppose that anyone would ever take moral judgments seriously. This, I think, is one reason why certain critics of this sort of analysis have claimed that it makes no sense of, and is essentially destructive of, morality, a charge that defenders of the theory have professed themselves unable to understand. But if this last point is correct, as I believe it is, then this sort of analysis does have moral implications, and is not morally neutral, as it is alleged and intended to be.

VI

I would not be understood as denying the importance of attitudes and feelings, not even their moral importance.[17] They are of considerable importance. They affect the way we view things, the way we react to things, and the ways in which we get along with others, and are thus among the most important elements of our lives. Purely intellectual analyses of moral phenomena, which leave out the elements of attitudes and feelings, leave out an important aspect of the subject, and in emphasizing these factors the emotive or attitude theories seem to me to have made an important contribution.[18] (Another important contribution these theories have made lies in the stimulus they have provided to clearer and more accurate thought about the matter.) I am reminded here of the story of the married couple who confessed, after many years of marriage, that they had never had children because they didn't want anyone to know what they had been doing. This should illustrate the importance of attitudes. What I do deny is that attitudes or feelings are the sum and substance of moral judgments, and that moral judgments can be analyzed as merely expressing or reporting them.

Indeed, I have often been tempted to say: " 'Emotive meaning' has no meaning; it only has emotive meaning." I must confess that I am sorely tempted to say it right now, but I shall restrain myself from doing so. It would, no doubt, be very expressive, but it would not be true.

NOTES

[1]The substance of this essay was given as a lecture at Marquette University on February 8, 1971. There is, however, no one-to-one correspondence; there are things here that were not said there, and there are things said there that are not here. The lecture was given from notes, and I felt free to improvise. Yet the correspondence is sufficiently close to retain the concept of identity. Earlier versions of this lecture, never exactly the same, were presented at Brandeis University, the University of Houston, the University of Leicester, Wichita State University, and the Carnegie Summer Institute at Notre Dame University. I trust the transformations have been beneficial.

[2]W. D. Lamont, *Introduction to Green's Moral Philosophy* (London: George Allen and Unwin Ltd., 1934), p. 151, paraphrasing a remark in sec. 311, p. 373, of Thomas Hill Green, *Prolegomena to Ethics*, ed., A. C. Bradley, 5th ed. (Oxford: The Clarendon Press, 1906; 1st ed., 1883).

[3]*The Aristotelian Society, Supplementary Volume*, XLI (1967), p. 189.

[4]A. J. Ayer, *Language, Truth and Logic*, 2nd ed. (London: Victor Gollancz Ltd., 1948), p. 108. This book was first published in 1936. Since then its author's views have changed in a number of respects. In an article, "On the Analysis of Moral Judgments," *Horizon*, XX, 117 (1949), reprinted in his *Philosophical Essays* (London: Macmillan, 1954), Professor Ayer said: "As for the moral judgment itself, it may be regarded as expressing the attitude which the reasons given for it are calculated to provoke. To say, as I once did, that these moral judgments are merely expressive of certain feelings, feelings of approval or disapproval, is an over-simplification. The fact is rather that what may be described as moral attitudes consist in certain patterns of behavior, and that the expression of a moral judgment is an element in the pattern. The moral judgment expresses the attitude in the sense that it contributes to defining it. . . . " (p. 238)

[5]This point stems from Moore, though my elaboration of it is somewhat different from his. See G. E. Moore, *Ethics* (London: Oxford Univ. Press, 1947: 1st ed., 1912), p. 63.

[6]Floyd L. Ruch, *Psychology and Life*, 2nd ed. (Chicago: Scott, Foresman and Co., 1941), p. 464.

[7]This point was made by Broad in criticism of Hume. I do not regard it as applicable to Hume, but I do regard it as valid against the present theory. See C. D. Broad, *Five Types of Ethical Theory* (London: Kegan Paul, Trench, Trubner and Co., 1930), pp. 114–115.

[8]Ayer, *Language, Truth and Logic*, p. 107.

[9]*Ibid.*, p. 111.

[10]*Ibid.*, p. 110. Also especially interesting is Ayer's challenge: "If anyone doubts the accuracy of this account of moral disputes, let him try to construct even an imaginary argument on a question of value which does not reduce itself to an argument about a question of logic or about an empirical matter of fact. I am confident that he will not succeed in producing a single example. . . . " (p. 112). This has remarkable resemblance to Hume's challenge: "But if anyone should deny this universal resemblance, I know no way of convincing him, but by desiring him to shew a simple impression, that has not a correspondent idea, or a simple idea, that has not a correspondent impression. If he does not answer this challenge, as 'tis certain he cannot, we may from his silence and our own observation establish our conclusion." *A Treatise of Human Nature*, Bk. I, Pt. 1, Sec. i, par. 5.

[11]The disguised imperative theory was put forward by Carnap, in a simple-minded way, in *Philosophy and Logical Syntax* (London: Kegan Paul, 1935), pp. 23–25. But it is also incorporated in Ayer's essentially emotive analysis of moral judgments, *Language, Truth and Logic*, p. 108. W. D. Ross's objections strike me as conclusive : *Foundations of Ethics* (Oxford: The Clarendon Press, 1939), pp. 33–35; see also pp. 40–41.

[12]Ayer, *Language, Truth and Logic*, p. 108.

[13]C. L. Stevenson, *Ethics and Language* (New Haven: Yale Univ. Press, 1944), p. 22.

[14]"The Emotive Meaning of Ethical Terms," *Mind*, XLVI (1937), reprinted in Stevenson's *Facts and Values* (New Haven and London: Yale Univ. Press, 1963), pp. 10–31.

[15]Stevenson, *Ethics and Language*, pp. 92–93.

[16]Stevenson, *Facts and Values*, p. 30.

[17]The following definition of "attitude," taken from *Webster's Dictionary of Synonyms* (Springfield, Mass.: G. and C. Merriam Co., 1951), p. 633 (entry two under "position"), is worth pondering: "A personal or, sometimes, a group or communal point of view, especially one that is colored by personal or party feeling, is influenced by one's environment or the fashion of the moment, and is, on the whole, more the product of temperament or emotion than thought or conviction."

[18]Thus I am inclined to agree wholeheartedly with the following central point of Stevenson's philosophy: "Our ethical judgments represent our personality in all its complexity. However much they may be guided by a full use of our intelligence, they do not spring from the intellect alone." *Facts and Values*, p. 232.

MUST MORALITY PAY?
or
What Socrates Should Have Said to Thrasymachus[1]

ANTONY FLEW

I

" 'Listen then', he said, 'for I say that justice is
nothing else but the advantage of the stronger.' "[2]
It is with this bitter intervention from Thrasymachus,
occurring halfway through the first of its ten Books,
that Plato's *Republic* begins to come urgently alive.
For the remainder of Book I the Socrates of the dialogue asks questions and raises objections, while
Thrasymachus keeps urging that in fact the just
man, the good man, is by his very justice and goodness the destined victim of exploitation. Morality
demands sacrifices from individuals. Being moral,
therefore, is not to the advantage of the individual
who makes the sacrifices, but only to that of those
who contrive to profit from them. Justice is thus a
good thing not for oneself but for other people.

The arguments which Socrates deploys against
Thrasymachus duly silence him, but they satisfy no
one. So in Book II, after Thrasymachus has been
put down, the challenge is renewed by Glaucon and

Adeimantus. These two are well-born and well-bred young men, with none of the hacking cynicism of Thrasymachus. Already in Book I, after concluding one argument with "I do not, therefore, agree at all with the assertion of Thrasymachus that justice is the advantage of the stronger," Socrates has turned to Glaucon for support: "I attach much greater importance to the present position of Thrasymachus, that the life of the unjust man is superior to that of the just man. And you, Glaucon, which side do you take? Which seems to you to speak truer?" To this Glaucon replies firmly: "I, for my part, think that the life of the just man is more profitable."[3]

Immediately at the beginning of Book II Glaucon distinguishes between three kinds of good, and presses Socrates to say to which one being just belongs. The second of these kinds is that of those things "which we value both for themselves and for their consequences, such as, for example, thought and sight and health."[4] And it is, of course, here that Socrates wants to put being just, "among those things which he who would be blessed must love both for their own sake and for their consequences."[5]

So Glaucon, supported later by his brother Adeimantus, while insisting that he himself has no doubt but that this is indeed the truth, proceeds— *con brio!*—to try to deploy the most powerful possible opposing case. What they ask Socrates to do is to fill a felt need: "Yet what each of these, justice and injustice, does, on its own account by the force of its own nature, when hidden away from both gods and men in the heart of the person who possesses it, no one has ever thoroughly considered in prose or in poetry; nor has anyone proved beyond doubt that injustice is the greatest of evils that the soul contains within herself, and justice the greatest good."[6]

The whole of the rest of the *Republic* seems to be presented as an attempt by Socrates, here presumably only a mouthpiece for Plato, to show that justice is after all always advantageous to the just man himself, not merely to other people—that it is, in the often quoted original Greek words, an *oikeion* (intrinsic good), and not merely an *allotrion agathon* (extrinsic good). It is in response to this Glauconian challenge that Plato presents his vision of an ideal city ruled by an elite order of Guardians: the notorious Philosopher Kings whose knowledge of the Ideal Forms—the abstract essences of things—enables them to prescribe to the uninitiated vulgar the true, eternal, and authoritative standards. And it is through this vision of a Dorian city stately as a Dorian temple that Plato expounds his own answer to what is the official master question of the entire dialogue: "What is justice?" It is entirely appropriate to Glaucon's original specification of the second kind of good, to his selection of illustrations there, and to his later explanation of precisely what it is which he wants to hear from Socrates, that the latter's wide-ranging response should include—as it does—what must surely have been the first systematic presentation of the now trendily topical yet still altogether paradoxical thesis that all delinquency is an expression of psychological disorder.[7]

II

Nevertheless, just as no one is satisfied with the reply which Socrates gives to Thrasymachus in Book I, so no one ought to be content with the Platonic response of the remaining nine Books. One main and vitiating fault, which runs right through the *Republic*, is the failure fully to appreciate and to come to terms with the fundamental distinction between what is the case and what ought to be. Thus Thrasymachus appeals to his own excessively hard-bitten view of how things actually are, whereas Socrates rests a large part of his case upon claims which are more or less explicitly about what ought to be. No one seems to say or to see that this difference is crucial. Yet suppose we were to allow that Plato was right about what would be true in the supposedly ideal world of his visionary Republic. Still this all must be and is enormously different from this world, which is the world in and about which Thrasymachus launched his original challenge. Even the successive formulations of the Socratic counter-thesis appear to be infected to some extent with the same ruinous ambiguity. It is, surely, one thing to say "that the life of the just man is more advantageous," and rather another to affirm that being just is "among those things which he who would be blessed must love both for their own sake and for their consequences."

I do not, however, want in the present paper to say very much immediately and directly about what the *Republic* actually offers in response first to Thrasymachus and then later to Glaucon. Instead I propose to examine that first contribution on my own account, and to ask what Socrates should have said to Thrasymachus. So consider again his most often quoted sentence: "Listen then, . . . for I say that justice is nothing else but the advantage of the stronger."

Since this is offered as the knock-down contribution to an investigation which clearly is a search for a definition of the word "justice," it seems natural to construe it as intended to be precisely that. Cornford in his translation even goes so far as to render the passage: "Listen then . . . . What I say is that 'just'. . . means nothing but what is to the interest of the stronger party." He makes it clear that this is to be read unequivocally as a definition by putting the word "just" between inverted commas—a refinement for which, of course, the Greek provides no warrant. If this were indeed the interpretation intended by Plato, then it would become very quickly obvious that Thrasymachus has not grasped what is and is not relevant to establishing the correctness of a proposed definition. For he at once rejects with anger a suggestion from Socrates that he might perhaps be "maintaining . . . that if Polydamas the athlete is stronger than we are, and if oxmeat is advantageous for his body, this food will be advantageous and just . . . ."[8]

What Thrasymachus actually wants to say, he explains, is "that some states are ruled by dictators, others are democracies, and others are aristocracies. . . . And each form of government lays down laws for its own advantage, a democracy laws for the

benefit of the populace, a dictatorship laws for the
benefit of the dictator, and the others likewise. By
legislating in this way they make it plain that their
advantage is justice for their subjects, and they
punish anyone who gets out of line with this as a
lawbreaker and an unjust man. So this is what I
mean, you splendid fellow, that justice is in all states
the same, and it is the advantage of the established
government. For this, you agree, is strong; so that if
you work it out correctly justice is everywhere the
same—the advantage of the stronger."9

III

Socrates responds: "I now grasp what you mean.
Whether it is true or not I shall attempt to discover."
Before we in turn attempt to discover whether either
of them were in fact seized of the implications of
what Thrasymachus has just added, let us try treating his first intervention as a descriptive definition.
Then, certainly, the first objection raised by
Socrates is to the point, though it is a pity that he
added the inept and redundant final clause "for us
who are weaker than him," a clause which I was
careful to omit when quoting that objection in the
last paragraph but one.

As a descriptive definition, "Justice is . . . the advantage of the stronger" will not do at all: the
expression "the advantage of the stronger" trans-
parently is not equivalent in meaning to the word to
be defined, "justice." Suppose, for instance, that
someone maintains—as some people will—that the

one-party regime in some newly emerging country is energetically and effectively engaged in building a just and (of course) a socialist society. Such a tribute will no doubt be welcome at the top. It might even help to earn the writer his slice of the fat cake of official hospitality. But this popularity could not, surely, long survive his explanation that for him at least "a just society," if not "a socialist society," simply means "a society in which the interests of the stronger (here, obviously, the all-powerful Central Committee) prevail over all other claims." This may be, and no doubt is, the truth about many regimes in emerging countries—as well as about plenty in emerged countries too. It most certainly is not the truth about the accepted meaning of the word "justice."

The mistake, however, which Thrasymachus is here assumed to be making is no dull and lumpish gaffe. It deserves better than the incredulous reference to Polydamas the athlete with which Socrates would dismiss it. For what on the present interpretation Thrasymachus is saying is not just wrong, period. To define the word "justice" as "the advantage of the stronger" is not to say something which merely happens to be mistaken. It is to make a move which is radically, spectacularly, diametrically, and hence most illuminatingly wrong. For it is central to the notion of justice that to appeal to justice must be to appeal to standards and principles logically independent of all particular individual and group interests. Only and precisely insofar as the standards and principles of justice are thus independent of all particular interests can it be in principle possible for such standards and principles to provide impartial adjudication when those particular interests conflict. And, even where there is no immediate question of conflict of interest, it is only and precisely insofar as the standards and principles of justice are thus independent of all particular interests that it can be in principle possible to assess any and every claim of any such interest by reference to these very standards and principles.

This is something different from and additional to the now hackneyed point that a commendatory word cannot be adequately defined in terms of only neutral expressions. That hackneyed though nonetheless vital point is one which it would be a little tricky to drive home with Thrasymachus, since he wants to remove or even to reverse the commendatory force of the terms "justice" and "injustice." Socrates asks: "I suppose you call one of them a virtue and the other a vice?" "Is that likely, my dear good fellow? You must remember that I also contend that injustice is profitable, justice not." "Well, what else?" "The opposite."[10]

Such points about the commendatory force of moral terms are nowadays usually made by reference to that classical passage in Hume's *Treatise* where he insists upon a categorial distinction between "ought" and "is."[11] The present different and additional point was also in his own way seized upon by Hume. For in a rather less frequently quoted passage in the second *Enquiry* he urged another fundamental distinction: between certain non-moral words, which are definable in terms of particular interests, and moral words, which necessarily cannot be so defined.

This passage runs: "When a man denominates another his 'enemy,' his 'rival,' his 'antagonist,' his 'adversary,' he is understood to speak the language of self-love and to express sentiments peculiar to himself and arising from his particular circumstances and situation. But when he bestows on any man the epithets of 'vicious' or 'odious' or 'depraved,' he then speaks another language and expresses sentiments in which he expects all his audience are to concur with him. He must here, therefore, depart from his private and particular situation and must choose a point of view common to him with others: he must move some universal principle of the human frame and touch a string to which all mankind have an accord and symphony."[12]

In its other aspect, the aspect in which there is no immediate question of any conflict of interest, the same point is best made by referring to a famous passage in the *Euthyphro*. Plato's Socrates presses the question, in the particular case of holiness (or piety): "Is the holy loved by the gods because it is holy, or is it holy because it is loved by the gods?"[13] If "justice" were to be defined in terms of the interests or prescriptions of any temporary or permanent power group, then those interests and prescriptions could not be criticized by reference to the idea and ideal of justice. Since they would by that token be necessarily just, they could not be commended for in fact possessing the contingent merit of actually being just, nor yet denounced for in fact possessing the contingent demerit of actually being unjust. Insofar as "justice" is taken to mean "what our laws prescribe," there can be no question whether the enforcement of these prescriptions really always is justice.

But that is precisely not the moral sense of the word "justice." The present Section III, which interprets the first intervention of Thrasymachus as a suggested descriptive definition of that sense, can be concluded most elegantly by referring to the Melian Dialogue. This comes in the *History* of Thucydides, and is a dramatic reconstruction of exchanges between the representatives of a great power—Athens —and those of a tiny island state—Melos. The Athenians wished to subjugate with as little fuss as possible this neutralist state, which fell unambiguously within their traditional sphere of influence. In fact they did, when the dialogue was over, "normalize" the situation by an exercise of overwhelming military force. One might say—if one's longing for international appeasement is not too strong to permit such uncomfortable memories of 1968—that the Melian Dialogue is a report on a Cierna and Tisou of the Great Athenian Empire.

Now it is often and with reason suggested that Thrasymachus and Cleitophon in the *Republic*, and similar characters in other Platonic dialogues, are spokesmen for ideas which were already part of the contemporary intellectual scene, and, in particular, that these ideas are put forward by the Athenians in the Melian Dialogue.[14] But look at what those Athenians actually say to the present point. They begin by indicating the framework which they think appropriate to discussion between insiders: "We on our side will not offer a lengthy speech which no one would believe, with a lot of fine talk about how it is our right to have an empire because we defeated the Persians, or that we are coming against you now because we have been wronged; and we do not expect you to think to persuade us that the reason why you did not join our camp was that you are kith and kin of the Spartans who originally settled Melos, or that you have done us no injury."

After this 400's B.C. equivalent of dismissing appeals to services rendered in the Great Anti-Fascist War, and of eschewing calls for the promotion of "socialism with a human face," the Athenians go on: "Rather we expect you to try to do what is possible on the basis of the true thoughts of both parties, since you know and we know that it is part of the human condition to choose justice only when the balance of power is even, and those who have the advantage do what they have the power to do while the weak acquiesce." The Melians accept that they cannot here appeal to justice as such: "Well, we consider that it is expedient that you should not destroy something which is for the general good. (The word has to be 'expedient' since you have in this way laid down that we must speak of advantage rather than justice.)"[15]

IV

Section III deployed the decisive objection against all attempts to define the word "justice" in terms of the interests or prescriptions of any particular power group. Once that objection has been put and grasped, we are in position to notice and neutralize two potentially confusing modern English idioms. In both, a form of words is used which may suggest that an account of meaning is being given. But in both it is essential to our understanding of what is being said that these semantic suggestions should be false.

The first of these two idioms is that in which an epigram is presented as if it were a definition. If someone says, boringly, that the word "uncle" means "parent's brother or brother-in-law," then he really is offering a definition of the word "uncle," and a correct one at that. But when, in a perhaps rather smug way, you give us your favourite definition of the Roman genius as an infinite capacity for making drains, or of tanks as being armoured and mechanized fire-power, then you are really making remarks about the Roman genius and about tanks, and quite good ones too. You certainly are not explicating the meanings of the expression "the Roman genius" or of the word "tank," for your remarks could not be understood by anyone who did not already know who the Romans were and what the words "genius" and "tank" mean. Nor could they be relished as good remarks by someone who mistakenly believed them to be tautological.

The second and to us more important of these two

idioms is a great favourite with all cynics and de-
bunkers. Someone says with a sneer, for instance, that
"when that playboy talks about a spiritual and
purely Platonic relationship what he really means is
four legs in a bed," or that "when those capitalist
imperialists speak about safeguarding the rights of
small Asian peoples to self-determination, what they
really mean is defending their own investments."
The statements made in this idiom have point only
and precisely insofar as what their subjects are said
really to mean is not the meaning of what they are
said to be saying. For, if it were, then the debunker's
occupation would be gone. There would be no mask
of hypocrisy to tear off.

Since Thrasymachus knew only classical Greek,
not modern English, it was not, of course, open to
him to express himself exactly in either of these two
ways. But certainly anyone writing a new *Republic*
for contemporary English-speaking readers would
have his Thrasymachus breaking in to say that his
definition of justice (not "justice") is the advantage
of the stronger, and that when those in power talk
about justice what they really mean is their own
advantage. And what Plato's Thrasymachus actually did say should surely be construed with an
eye to the correct interpretation of these modern
idioms.

For, as we saw in Section II, immediately after
saying in best debunker's style "that justice is nothing else but the advantage of the stronger," Thrasymachus goes on to urge an empirical rather than
a conceptual thesis: that "each form of government

lays down laws for its own advantage, a democracy
laws for the benefit of the populace, a dictatorship
laws for the benefit of the dictator, and the others
likewise." As he continues, Thrasymachus finds himself employing giveaway phrases which suggest that
—whatever the truth of his empirical claims—the
word "justice" simply cannot be defined in terms
of the advantage of the stronger: "By legislating in
this way they make it plain that their advantage is
justice for their subjects, and they punish anyone
who gets out of line with this as a lawbreaker and
an unjust man. For if the mere fiat of the rulers were
sufficient to make something just there would, surely,
be no call for him to add "for their subjects," and
his "they punish anyone who gets out of line with
this as . . . an unjust man" at least hints at a sup-
pressed "as if he were."

Nevertheless, it would be entirely wrong to suggest that any of this is clear to Thrasymachus himself. The development of the ensuing discussion
shows that neither Thrasymachus nor Socrates within the dialogue nor, presumably, Plato outside com-
posing it, is a thorough master of the distinction
between contentions about the meanings of words
and theses about supposed matters of fact and real
existence. For, after Thrasymachus has explained
himself by saying things which suggest that he wants
to maintain a thesis about the actual behaviour of
men in power, Socrates responds, not by appealing
to counter-examples, which would show that the
true political picture is not in fact as unrelievedly
black as that painted by Thrasymachus, but by

objecting that rulers may by mistake command what happens in fact not to be in their interests. To this Thrasymachus replies, not by accepting the modest amendment proposed by Cleitophon—to say that those in power command not what is but what they believe to be in their own interests—but by going into a Conventionalist Sulk and proposing a high redefinition of "ruler," such that a ruler is only truly a ruler insofar as he makes no mistakes.[16] This in turn encourages Socrates, who has shown no signs of needing much encouragement, to go on about how (true) rulers are definitionally concerned only with the good of their subjects. And so on.

The lesson for us to draw is one which the *Republic* itself does not know to teach. It is that the sort of debunking thesis urged by Thrasymachus should not be construed as offering a semantic analysis of the ideas to be debunked. Instead it claims to reveal what actually is going on behind the fine talk; and this, if the whole is to be an exercise in debunking, must necessarily be something very different.[17] One illuminating comparison here would be with anthropologists' accounts of the actual working of social institutions which essentially involve erroneous ideas. A full understanding of the institution of taboo, for instance, or of the igurramen among the Berbers, requires three things: first, a mastery of these ideas—the ideas in terms of which the participants both operate and misunderstand the institution; second, a knowledge of what actually is and is not going on; and, third, an appreciation of why this is not and cannot be what the participants themselves believe is going on.[18]

V

However, as we saw back in Section I, it is not the
political analysis of Thrasymachus which most immediately concerns Socrates— and, presumably,
Plato. It is the consequence which Thrasymachus
wants to derive from that and other similar analyses:
"that the life of the unjust man is superior to that of
the just man." This conclusion Thrasymachus founds
upon the contention that to be just involves sacrificing one's own interests to those of other people, a
contention which is in turn taken to warrant the
further inference that the man who chooses to be
just must be a fool: "You must see, my most simple
Socrates, that the just man always comes off worse
than the unjust. Consider first commercial dealings,
when a just and an unjust man are partners. You
will not find at the dissolution of the partnership
that the just man ever has more than the unjust, but
less. Then again in dealings with the state, when
there are taxes to pay out of equal incomes the just
man pays more, the unjust less. And, when it is a
matter of taking, the one gains nothing, the other
plenty."[19]

Thrasymachus states and overstates his case with
cynical ferocity. He presses home the immoral moral
that justice is, therefore, "a right noble simplicity,"
while injustice, if not perhaps exactly a virtue, certainly is "good policy."[20] This is the challenge
which shocked Plato's Socrates, and which has gone

on shocking generations of readers of the *Republic*. Yet any satisfactory response to Thrasymachus must begin by stating emphatically and categorically that on his basic point he is right. For, as we saw in Section III, it is of the essence of morality in general and of justice in particular that they must, in anything less than an ideal world, from time to time demand sacrifices.

That this is indeed the case is precisely one mark which distinguishes this, our world, as not-ideal. So one way in which some people strive to make it somewhat less not-ideal is by establishing penal and other institutions, part of the function of which is to supply artificial incentives through which conduct which would otherwise be virtuous but not prudent may become prudent as well as virtuous. Only given the perfect enforcement of a system in which penalties were perfectly adjusted to both offenses and offenders would it be true that crime never pays. Even then, as any liberal must insist, there would be many offenses which were immoral but not criminal. So with regard to at least some of these we should still have to ask: "Is it for nothing that people have wondered for so long why the wicked prosper?"[21]

It is, therefore, radically misguided for Plato's Socrates to attempt to deny the Thrasymachean claim that in fact in this actual world morality often does demand sacrifices; and it is also, of course, unsound in method to try to meet his point about the actual world by appealing to what perhaps would be the case in another possible world. It is equally but more interestingly misguided in method here to inquire into the nature of justice by examining it first, writ large as it were, in a just collective: "So, if you agree, let us investigate its nature first in states, and only after this look at it in the individual too, searching for the likeness of the greater in the form of the less."[22]

This insidiously persuasive suggestion is, once again, diametrically wrong. For Thrasymachus has not disputed, or at any rate he has no need to dispute, that justice makes for the common good, that an observance by everybody of its dictates is in the collective interest. What such a cautious Thrasymachus is concerned to underline is that what is in the collective interest is not always and necessarily in the individual interests of members of that collective; and this is true. The truth—and it is a truth which the whole method of Plato's Socrates seems calculated to conceal—is that morality often does demand sacrifices, and when it does, then it is not profitable to oneself but, at best, to others. It is preposterous to try to pretend that, if I can get away with not paying my fair share of some general levy, this evasion, which quite certainly harms the collective, cannot be to my individual advantage.

It is a consequence of what was said in Section III about the impossibility of defining the word "justice" in terms of any particular interest, that there can be no necessary coincidence between my individual duty and my individual advantage. Insofar as there is such a coincidence between the dictates of a purely self-interested prudence and the demands

of decency and morality, this can be a matter not of
logically necessary connection but only of fortunate
contingent fact. Had there been, either in fact or
necessarily, a perfect congruence between the two
it is hard to see how we could have come to employ
—and so often to contrast—the notions both of
prudence and of morality. The two could have been
equated or identified as one within a dream system
so perfect that no one would have needed to be
good. That this is not how it is in fact can be fixed
finally by thinking of what we all—and rightly—
think of the wretch who upon absolutely every occa-
sion discovers a most convenient identity between
his own self-interest and the requirements of duty.[23]

VI

The main would-be factual point of Thrasymachus has, therefore, simply to be accepted, although
there certainly is need to moderate and to qualify
the cynical extremism of his presentation. But there
is another and more philosophical task still to be
started. We have to challenge the assumption that
the main thesis, that morality often calls for sacrifices, carries the implications: first, that anyone who
knowingly makes such sacrifices must be a fool;
and, second, "that the life of the unjust man is
superior to that of the just man."

The reason why it does not follow, from the fact
that some course of action would involve self-sacri-
fice, that it must be irrational knowingly to choose
that course and to make that sacrifice, is that no

desire and no choice can as such be either rational
or irrational. To choose to act in this way rather
than that may be usual or unusual, to be encouraged
or to be discouraged. But it is itself no more either
rational or irrational than it is rational or irrational
to like or dislike kippers or to prefer daughters to
sons or sons to daughters. Questions about these
philosophically high-toned alternatives, rational or
irrational, arise only when we come to examine the
coherence of plans and purposes, or the internal
consistency of some proposed justification for one
course or preference as opposed to another: when,
for instance, we notice that people who have set
themselves some objective nevertheless persist in
doing things which they cannot fail to recognize
must frustrate their own chosen purposes, or when
some ingenuous addlepate offers as his reasons for
one course of action considerations which should
have led him to do the very opposite.

This is another lesson which we ought to have
learned from Hume: a choice is, in itself, no more
rational or irrational than is a desire. And if anyone
would challenge Hume by insisting that it is good
colloquial English to commend certain approved
desires and choices as reasonable, and their rejection
as unreasonable, then it has to be pointed out that
the senses of "reasonable" and "unreasonable" here
are either quite different from those just indicated,
or else reducible to them. In the latter case the
present objection collapses. In the former they must
be entirely non-intellectual, and hence irrelevant.
It is still far too often assumed, both by "men of the

world" and by the world-rejecting authors of text-
books of moral theology, that it is paradigmatically
rational for a man singlemindedly to pursue his
own long-term self-interest.[24] Yet it just is not, at
least in the relevant intellectual sense of "rational."
Nor correspondingly, is it necessarily irrational to
choose, quite deliberately, to sacrifice possible but
unfair gains. To be scrupulous is not, as such, to be
a fool.

Again, since the claim "that the life of the unjust
man is superior to that of the just man" is presumably a commendation, it cannot be derived
directly and exclusively from the purely factual contention that the latter may involve sacrifices not
required by the former. And, unless this factual contention is part of the meaning of that claim, it must
be possible consistently to reject the claim, and to
commend instead the life of the just man, while
nevertheless accepting the prime thesis of Thrasymachus. It seems, therefore, that Philippa Foot was
wrong to say that "if justice is not a good to the just
man, moralists who recommend it as a virtue are
perpetrating a fraud."[25]

What would indeed be a fraud would be to recommend justice on the grounds that justice must necessarily pay, and be always in the interests of the just
man himself. Also, for the same reason, it would be
a fraud to rate justice "among those things which
he who would be blessed must love both for their
own sake and for their consequences"—unless, of
course, this thesis is itself to be read not merely as
partly but as purely normative. In this implausible

reading what is being said is that we ought to love justice for its own sake and for its consequences, regardless of any questions whether, either necessarily or contingently, these consequences chime with our own particular and individual interests.

Any commendation which is not to be a fraud will have to concentrate on praising just acts as such, and to mention consequences, if at all, only insofar as these are good regardless of whether they are good for the agent himself. This will presumably be a matter of saying that such acts are fine, and that the alternatives are just out because—as Browning had it—"there is a decency required," adding perhaps that justice makes for the common good.

Considerations of this kind most surely will not satisfy Thrasymachus. But then what is he, and what are we, looking for? We cannot show him that he is wrong in insisting that the dictates of morality often contradict the indications of prudence. For in fact they do. Now, if in any such conflict he systematically prefers the latter, and has no general concern about morality as such, or indeed about anything but his own particular interests, then he will not be interested in whatever we may say about things which are good but not good for him. Yet to take this stance is exactly what Thrasymachus is for. He is the archetypal spokesman for a pure self-interestedness. He makes no serious or ingenuous claim to be moral, but only to be both realistic and rational. Certainly he can be faulted for being rather more cynical than realistic, and for exaggerating the truth which he has seized. But he cannot be said to be irrational in his actual preferences. A man may be rational but not virtuous, and professionally, Thrasymachus is rational. Since preferences as such, and the ultimate choice of a way of life, are not in themselves either rational or irrational, how could we make out that his preferences, and his choice, are in themselves irrational, any more than he in his turn could prove that they are rational? The ideas of rationality and of irrationality find no purchase at this point.

NOTES

[1]A first version of this paper was given as a talk on the Third Program of the British Broadcasting Corporation, and later printed in *The Listener* (October 16, 1966).

[2]*Republic*, 338C. This and all later translations from the Greek are mine.

[3]*Ibid.*, 347E.

[4]*Ibid.*, 357C.

[5]*Ibid.*, 358A.

[6]*Ibid.*, 366E.

[7]See Anthony Kenny, "Mental Health in Plato's *Republic*," *Proceedings of the British Academy*, (1969); and compare especially Part One of my *Crime or Disease?* (London: Macmillan, 1973).

[8]*Republic*, 338C-D.

[9]*Ibid.*, 338E–339A.

[10]*Ibid.*, 348C.

[11]See for discussion of this W. D. Hudson, ed., *The Is-Ought Question* (New York: St. Martin's Press, 1969).

[12]*An Enquiry Concerning the Principles of Morals*, IX, i: here and elsewhere punctuation has been altered to conform with the style followed in the rest of this paper.

[13]*Euthyphro*, 9E ff. It is well to emphasize here that it is Plato's Socrates who is speaking. For this basic distinction is being developed in the course of an argument intended to discredit Euthyphro; and, as Professor Geach has recently reminded us, the offense of Euthyphro is that he is proposing to prosecute his own father for being responsible for the death of man who was nothing but a farm laborer. It is permissible to hope that the historical Socrates did not share the aristocratic callousness suggested by Plato's Socrates in this dialogue. See P. T. Geach, *God and the Soul* (London: Routledge and Kegan Paul, 1969), pp. 117–119.

[14]See, for example, Lord Lindsay's introduction to the Everyman edition: *The Republic of Plato*, ed. and trans., A. D. Lindsay (New York: Dutton, 1935), pp. xix-xxi.

[15]Thucydides, *History*, V, 89.

[16]Several colleagues have been good enough to attribute the introduction of the phrase "Conventionalist Sulk" to me: see, for instance, Geach, p. 3. But my own fallible recollection is that this is not one of my coinages, and that it was first used by David Pears while we were both Lecturers at Christ Church, Oxford in 1949–50. "High redefinition" and "low redefinition" both come from Paul Edwards. They are to be found in his "Bertrand Russell's Doubts about Induction," reprinted in *Logic and Language*, First Series, ed., Antony Flew (Oxford: Blackwell, 1951).

[17]The hermeneutic ideas developed in this Section IV may, I suggest, with appropriate alterations be applied to the passage in *A Treatise of Human Nature* where Hume says: "So that when you pronounce any action or character to be vicious, you mean nothing, but that from the constitution of your nature you have a feeling or sentiment of blame from the contemplation of it. Vice and virtue, therefore, may be compared to sounds, colors, heat and cold, which according to modern philosophy, are not qualities in objects, but perceptions in the mind. And this discovery in morals, like that other in physics, is to be regarded as a considerable advancement of the speculative sciences . . . . " (III, i, 1).

[18]See, for instance, my "Anthropology and Rationality," *Question No. 5* (London: Pemberton, 1972). This is a critical notice of Bryan Wilson, ed., *Rationality* (Oxford: Blackwell, 1971).

[19]*Republic*, 343D-E.

[20]*Ibid.*, 348C-D.

[21]D. Z. Phillips, "Does it Pay to be Good?" *Proceedings of the Aristotelian Society*, 1964–65, p. 47; compare chs. II-III of his *Death and Immortality* (London: Macmillan, 1970).

[22]*Republic*, 369A.

[23]Compare, for instance, famous passages of the *Treatise* in II, iii, 3 and III, i, 1.

[24]A view of this kind is maintained by P. T. Geach, ch. IX. For criticism compare again D. Z. Phillips. When Phillips speaks of the unjust man through his injustice ruining his soul, albeit in a sense carrying no implications of any future life of rewards and punishments, it seems that he has still not totally abandoned the notion that injustice must necessarily be against the interests of the unjust man himself, a notion which, seen in Geach, Phillips excoriates. If this is correct, or even if it is not, what Phillips here and elsewhere labors to present, by persuasive definition, as "true religion" is a compromise formation: on the one hand is the faith of the Saints and of the Fathers, of the Popes and of the Councils, which for good philosophical reasons he would totally reject; on the other hand are certain major consequences of the truth of that historic faith which Phillips, for whatever more private reasons, wishes still to retain. One bizarre fruit of this ill-starred commitment is that Phillips is apt to accuse others who—like Geach and me—argue about the implications and presuppositions of the traditional faith, of being scandalously ignorant of what "true religion" is. The truth is that we are both familiar with Phillipsism, but we both—though approaching from opposite sides—usually prefer to attend to Christianity as traditionally lived and preached.

[25]"Moral Beliefs," *Proceedings of the Aristotelian Society*, 1958–59, p. 100. Mrs. Foot, I believe, has more recently changed her mind on this point.

BIOGRAPHICAL NOTES

William Frankena received his A.B. from Calvin College in 1930, his A.M. from the University of Michigan in 1931, and his Ph.D. from Harvard in 1937. He has been Professor of Philosophy at the University of Michigan since 1947 and was chairman of the department during 1947-1961. He is a recipient of the Guggenheim Fellowship and is past president of the American Philosophical Association. He has been Visiting Professor of Philosophy at many universities, including Harvard in 1955 and again in 1962-63. Presently, Professor Frankena is preparing The Paul Carus Foundation Lectures. As a scholar, he is known for his many publications in ethics and philosophy of education. His books are *Ethics*, 1963; *Philosophy of Education*, 1965; *Three Historical Philosophies of Education*, 1965; and *Some Beliefs About Justice*, 1966. He has also published numerous articles in various philosophical journals and anthologies.

Marcus Singer received his A.B. from the University of Illinois in 1948 and his Ph.D. from Cornell University in 1952. He has been Professor of Philosophy at the University of Wisconsin, Madison since 1963 and was chairman of the department during 1963-1968. He is a recipient of the Guggenheim Fellowship and many other honors. He was Visiting Professor of Philosophy at Carleton College in the fall 1972-73 session. He has contributed many articles to various philosophical journals and anthologies. Among his publications are: *Generalization In Ethics*, 1961; *Introductory Readings in Philosophy*, 2nd ed. scheduled for December, 1973; *Reason and the Common Good: Selected Essays of Arthur E. Murphy,* 1963; *Belief, Knowledge, and Truth: Readings in the Theory of Knowledge,* 1970.

Antony Flew received his B.A. from St. John's College in Oxford, England in 1947 and his M.A. in 1949. He was Professor of Philosophy in the University of Keele from 1954-1971. He has been Visiting Professor of Philosophy at the Universities of Maryland, New York at Buffalo, and Southern California for the respective sessions of the 1970-71 academic year. He is presently finishing a temporary appointment as Professor of Philosophy at the University of Calgary, after which he will return to England to be Professor of Philosophy at the University of Reading. Among his many publications are: *A New Approach to Psychical Research,* 1953; *Hume's Philosophy of Belief,* 1961; *God and Philosophy,* 1966; *Evolutionary Ethics,* 1967; *An Introduction to Western Philosophy,* 1971; *Crime or Disease?,* 1973. Professor Flew has also edited several books and has published numerous articles in various philosophical journals and anthologies.

Curtis L. Carter received his A.B. from Taylor University in 1960 and his Ph.D. from Boston University in 1971. He is currently Assistant Professor of Philosophy at Marquette University and has been Visiting Assistant Professor of Philosophy at the University of Wisconsin, Milwaukee. He is a recipient of several fellowships, including a National Endowment of the Arts Critic's Fellowship, and has published in the *Journal of Aesthetics and Art Criticism* and other journals.

SUGGESTED READINGS

Books

AIKEN, HENRY DAVID. *Reason and Conduct.* New York: Alfred A. Knopf, Inc., 1962.

AYER, A. J. *Language Truth, and Logic.* 2nd ed. London: Victor Gollancz Ltd., 1948. Ch. 6.

BAIER, KURT. *The Moral Point of View: A Rational Basis of Ethics.* Ithaca: Cornell University Press, 1958.

BRANDT, RICHARD B. *Ethical Theory.* Englewood Cliffs, N.J.: Prentice-Hall, 1961.

EDWARDS, PAUL. *The Logic of Moral Discourse.* New York: The Free Press, 1955.

GAUTHIER, D. *Practical Reasoning.* London: Oxford University Press, 1963.

GINSBERG, MORRIS. *On the Diversity of Morals.* New York: The Macmillan Company, 1956.

HAZLITT, HENRY. *The Foundations of Morality.* Princeton, N.J.: Van Nostrand, 1964. Ch. 23.

KERNER, GEORGE C. *The Revolution in Ethical Theory.* London: Oxford University Press, 1966.

MONRO, D. H. *Empiricism and Ethics.* Cambridge: The University Press, 1967.

MOSER, SHIA. *Absolutism and Relativism in Ethics.* Springfield, Ill.: Charles C. Thomas Publisher, 1968.

PRICHARD, H. A. *Moral Obligation.* Oxford: The Clarendon Press, 1949.

ROSS, W. D. *The Right and the Good.* Oxford: The Clarendon Press, 1930.

SINGER, MARCUS GEORGE. *Generalization in Ethics.* New York: Alfred A. Knopf, Inc., 1961.

STEVENSON, C. L. *Ethics and Language.* New Haven: Yale University Press, 1944.

_____. *Facts and Values.* New Haven: Yale University Press, 1963.

TAYLOR, PAUL. *Normative Discourse.* Englewood Cliffs, N.J.: Prentice-Hall, 1961.

_____. *Problems of Moral Philosophy: An Introduction to Ethics.* Belmont, Calif.: Dickenson Publishing Company, 1967. Chs. 2–3.

TOULMIN, STEPHEN. *The Place of Reason in Ethics.* Cambridge: The University Press, 1950.

URMSON, J. O. *The Emotive Theory of Ethics.* London: Oxford University Press, 1969.

VEATCH, HENRY. *For an Ontology of Morals.* Evanston: Northwestern University Press, 1971.

WARNOCK, G. J. *Contemporary Moral Philosophy.* New York: St. Martin's Press, 1967. Ch. 5.

WARNOCK, MARY. *Ethics Since 1900.* London: Oxford University Press, 1960.

WESTERMARCK, EDVARD. *Ethical Relativity.* Westport, Conn.: Greenwood Press, 1970.

Articles

ANSCOMBE, G. E. M. "Modern Moral Philosophy," *Philosophy,* XXXIII (1958), pp. 97–110.

BLACK, MAX. "Some Questions About Emotive Meaning," *The Philosophical Review*, LXIII (1964), pp. 165–181.

BLAKE, RALPH M. "The Ground of Moral Obligation," *Ethics*, XXXVIII (1927–1928), pp. 129–140.

BLANSHARD, BRAND. "The New Subjectivism in Ethics," *Philosophy and Phenomenological Research*, IX (1949), pp. 504–511.

BRANDT, R. B. "The Emotive Theory of Ethics," *The Philosophical Review*, LIX (1950), pp. 305–318.

BRUNTON, J. A. "Egoism and Morality," *Philosophical Quarterly*, VI (1956), pp. 289–303.

_____. "Restricted Moralities," *Philosophy*, XLI (1966), pp. 113–126.

DURRANT, R. G. "Moral Neutrality and the Analysis of Morality," *Australasian Journal of Philosophy*, XXXVI (1958), pp. 169–188.

EVELING, H. S. "Some Patterns of Justification in Ethics," *Proceedings of the Aristotelian Society*, LXVI (1965–1966), pp. 149–166.

FINDLAY, J. N. "The Methodology of Normative Ethics," *Journal of Philosophy*, LVIII (1961), pp. 757–764.

_____. "Morality by Convention," *Mind*, LIII (1944), pp. 142–169.

FIRTH, R. "Ethical Absolutism and the Ideal Observer," *Philosophy and Phenomenological Research*, XII (1952), pp. 317–345.

FLEW, ANTONY. "On Deriving 'Ought' from 'Is'," *Analysis*, XXV (1964), pp. 25–32.

FOOT, P. R. "In Defence of the Hypothetical Imperative," *Philosophic Exchange*, I (1971), pp. 137–145.

_____, and JONATHAN HARRISON. "When Is a Principle a Moral Principle?" (Symposium), *Proceedings of the Aristotelian Society*, Suppl. XXVIII (1954), pp. 95–134.

FRANKENA, W. K. "Ethical Naturalism Renovated," *Review of Metaphysics,* X (1957), pp. 459–473.

_____. "MacIntyre on Defining Morality," *Philosophy* XXXIII (1958), pp. 158–162.

_____. "On Saying the Ethical Thing," *Proceedings and Addresses of the American Philosophical Association,* XXXIX (1965–1966), pp. 21–42.

_____. "The Concept of Morality," *University of Colorado Studies* (1965), pp. 1–22.

_____. "Recent Conceptions of Morality," in *Morality and the Language of Conduct,* eds. H. N. Castaneda and G. Nakhnikian (Detroit: Wayne State University Press, 1961), pp. 1–24.

GAUTHIER, DAVID P. "Morality and Advantage," *The Philosophical Review,* LXXVI (1967), pp. 460–475.

GELLNER, E. A. "Ethics and Logic," *Proceedings of the Aristotelian Society,* LV (1954–1955), pp. 157–158.

GERWIRTH, ALAN. "Metaethics and Moral Neutrality," *Ethics,* LXXVIII (1968), pp. 214–225. (A reply to Sumner)

GRIFFITHS, A. P., and R. S. PETERS. "The Autonomy of Prudence," *Mind,* LXXI (1953), pp. 161-180.

HARRISON, JONATHAN, and R. F. HOLLAND. "Moral Scepticism" (Symposium), *Proceedings of the Aristotelian Society,* Suppl. XLI (1967), pp. 185–214.

_____. "Self-Interest and Duty," *Australasian Journal of Philosophy,* XXXI (1953), pp. 22–29.

_____, and H. D. LEWIS. "The Autonomy of Ethics" (Symposium), *Proceedings of the Aristotelian Society,* Suppl. XXXII (1958), pp. 25–74.

HORSBURGH, H. J. N. "Criteria of Assent to a Moral Rule," *Mind,* LXII (1954), pp. 345–368.

JARVIS, J. "In Defense of Moral Absolutes," *Journal of Philosophy,* LV (1958), pp. 1043–1053.

KALIN, JESSE. "Baier's Refutation of Ethical Egoism," *Philosophical Studies*, XXII (1971), pp. 75–78.

_____. "In Defense of Ethical Egoism," in *Morality and Rational Self-Interest*, ed. David P. Gauthier (Englewood Cliffs, N.J.: Prentice-Hall, 1970), pp. 64–87.

KLUCKHOLN, CLYDE. "Ethical Relativity: Sic et Non," *Journal of Philosophy*, LII (1955), pp. 663–677.

LADD, J. "The Desire to Do One's Duty for Its Own Sake," in *Morality and the Language of Conduct*, pp. 301–349.

MACINTYRE, ALASDAIR. "What Morality Is Not," *Philosophy*, XXXII (1957), pp. 325–335.

MARGOLIS, JOSEPH. " 'Moral' and 'Rational'," *The Journal of Value Inquiry*, VI (1972), pp. 286–293.

MEDLIN, B. "Ultimate Principles and Ethical Egoism," *Australasian Journal of Philosophy*, XXXV (1957), pp. 111–118.

MEILAND, J. W. "Duty and Interest," *Analysis*, XXIII (1963), pp. 106–110.

MELDEN, A. I. "Why Be Moral?" *Journal of Philosophy*, XLV (1948), pp. 449–456.

NIELSEN, KAI. "Anthropology and Ethics," *The Journal of Value Inquiry*, V (1971), pp. 253–266.

_____. "Appraising Doing the Thing Done," *Journal of Philosophy*, LVII (1960), pp. 749–759.

_____. "Is 'Why Should I be Moral?' an Absurdity?" *Australasian Journal of Philosophy*, XXXVI (1958), pp. 25–32.

_____. "On Moral Truth," in *Studies in Moral Philosophy: American Philosophical Quarterly Monograph Series*, No. 1, ed. Nicholas Rescher (Oxford: Basil Blackwell, 1968), pp. 9–25.

_____. "Why Should I Be Moral?" *Methodos*, XV (1963), pp. 275–306.

PHILLIPS, D. Z. "Does it Pay to be Good?" *Proceedings of the Aristotelian Society*, LXV (1964–1965), pp. 45–60.

PHILLIPS, G. A. "Acting with Reason," *Philosophical Quarterly*, VII (1958), pp. 289–299.

_____. "Justifying Moral Principles," *Proceedings of the Aristotelian Society*, LVII (1957–1958), pp. 103–124.

PRICHARD, H. A. "Does Moral Philosophy Rest on a Mistake?" *Mind*, XXI (1912), pp. 21–37.

RACHELS, JAMES. "Evaluating From a Point of View," *The Journal of Value Inquiry*, VI (1972), pp. 144–157.

REES, W. J. "Moral Rules and the Analysis of 'Ought'," *The Philosophical Review*, LXII (1953), pp. 23–40.

ROBERTS, GEORGE. "Some Refutations of Private Subjectivism in Ethics," *The Journal of Value Inquiry*, V (1971), pp. 292–309.

ROBINSON, R. "The Emotive Theory of Ethics," *Proceedings of the Aristotelian Society*, Suppl. XXII (1948), pp. 79–106.

SPRIGGE, TIMOTHY L. S. "Definition of Moral Judgment," *Philosophy*, XXXIX (1964), pp. 301–322.

STEVENSON, C. L. "Brandt's Questions about Emotive Ethics," *The Philosophical Review*, LIX (1950), pp. 528–534.

_____. "Persuasive Definitions," *Mind*, LXXI (1962), pp. 331–350.

STOCKS, J. L. "Is There a Moral End?" *Proceedings of the Aristotelian Society*, Suppl. VIII (1928), pp. 62–75.

SUMNER, L. W. "Normative Ethics and Metaethics," *Ethics*, LXXVII (1967), pp. 95–106. (A reply to Gerwith)

TAYLOR, PAUL. "Social Science and Ethical Relativism," *Journal of Philosophy*, LV (1958), pp. 32–44.

_____. "The Ethnocentric Fallacy," *The Monist*, XLVII (1963), pp. 563–584.

THORTON, J. C. "Can the Moral Point of View Be Justified?" *Australasian Journal of Philosophy*, XLII (1964), pp. 22–34.

TOULMIN, S. E. "Principles of Morality," *Philosophy*, XXI (1956), pp. 142–153.

WADIA, P. A. "Why Should I Be Moral?" *Australasian Journal of Philosophy*, XLII (1964), pp. 216–226.

WALL, G. "Perspectives on the Objectivity of Moral Judgments," *Journal of Thought*, VI (1971), pp. 248–253.

WELLMAN, CARL. "Ethics Since 1950," *The Journal of Value Inquiry*, VI (1972), pp. 83–90.

WERTHEIM, PETER. "Morality and Advantage," *Australasian Journal of Philosophy*, XLII (1964), pp. 375–387.

WINCH, PETER. "Can a Good Man be Harmed?" *Proceedings of the Aristotelian Society*, LXVI (1965–1966), pp. 55–70.

_____. "Understanding a Primitive Society," in *Religion and Understanding*, ed. D. Z. Phillips (Oxford: Basil Blackwell, 1967), pp. 37–42.

INDEX